Journey for Margaret

By the same author

WHAT PEOPLE SAID

W. L. WHITE

Journey for Margaret

HARCOURT, BRACE AND COMPANY, NEW YORK

CONTENTS

1. PROCESSIONAL   3
2. DESTROYER   5
3. WHERE IS THE WAR?   24
4. MARGARET: I   37
5. WOMEN IN HELMETS   52
6. I AM BLOWN UP   56
7. MARGARET: II   67
8. THE ROAD TO THE CROSSES   76
9. RIDING THE FIRE-WAGONS   110
10. MARGARET: III   116
11. NIGHT LIFE   120
12. MARGARET: IV   124
13. DEATH IN THE DARK   126
14. MARGARET: V   167
15. MINE-SWEEPER   173
16. MARGARET: VI   198
17. LONDON FIRE   202
18. MARGARET: VII   230
19. RECESSIONAL   235

Journey for Margaret

1. PROCESSIONAL

FIFTY-SEVEN, fifty-eight, fifty-nine! And now the new inflatable rubber mattress, stretched out on our New York living-room floor, is full. Won't hold another lungful of air.

In this last desperate rush of emergency packing, this little toy from Abercrombie and Fitch is the last thing I've bought. I haven't seen London since the heavy raids, but I have a notion I'll need it to get real sleep on basement floors, subway platforms, gutters, or whatever you use for shelter there.

But here I am—fiddling with this gadget, while I let Kathrine wrestle with the real packing—trying to get my tin hat, gas mask, aluminum typewriter and enough shirts and sox into the big waterproof Norwegian rucksack. This mad rush began two hours ago when a cable came from the London agents. They said I should immediately get in touch with the British port officer in command of a Canadian port which I can't name.

So I called him long distance and he said, guardedly, that if I could catch a plane and be there by noon tomorrow, they could provide me with an "unusual means" of transportation to London.

Kathrine assumes they will take me over on one of the fifty over-age destroyers we've just turned over to them. I say nothing. But I'm carefully keeping my total luggage cut down to airplane weight. Because aren't they just beginning to fly American bombers over the Atlantic?

Then there's a small item of purely personal business. "Darling," says Kathrine, as she packs darned sox tight around the old Swedish gas mask, "when you get to London, why not look into the chances of adopting some children?"

We'd always been talking about it and somehow never had. Maybe couldn't quite afford it, or were scared by the things we heard. You had to apply, get approved, then you waited. Months always, sometimes years, before your turn came. Then if you didn't like what was pushed out at you over the counter, you could refuse—and wait more months or years.

"With the war," Kathrine continues, "and all the orphans and refugees—surely there must be some child there—anyway it can't be as bad as it is here—not so long to wait."

She might have something there. Just to make sure it wouldn't slip my mind in London, I wrote a little note to myself in cablese in my memorandum book: "UPLOOK KIDS."

[4]

2. DESTROYER

NOW we are out of harbor heading into open sea. The Canadian coast drops away through the porthole of the wardroom where I lunch with these six British officers who are taking one of the former American destroyers over to England. I can't tell you her name. I can't name the Canadian port. I couldn't then have told you the name of the British port we were bound for; not our captain, not even the British Admiralty, knew it. London would decide it later when we were a few days off the British coast, according to the prevalence of submarines and dive bombers. Our orders were to proceed to a penciled dot on the vast chart of the tossing Atlantic and there await instructions.

At this first lunch the captain, the first lieutenant, the chief engineer officer, the gunnery officer and the pink two sub-lieutenants at the table were as alike as well-groomed peas in a steel pod. They were to emerge as individuals later.

"I say," said the youngest sub, "did you hear what Jerry's saying about us?"

[5]

"No," said the first officer. "What are they saying?"

"That we jolly well won't get through."

"Where'd you hear that?" asked chief, which is short for chief engineer officer.

"Guns told me. Wireless room told him—didn't they, Guns?"

"So they did," said the gunnery officer. "They always listen to the German wireless. Happened to pick this up half an hour ago. Seemed to think he knew all about us —what port we were leaving, when, and everything. Could I trouble you for the cream?"

"Jerry's always boasting. Remember they threatened to be in London by August 15th," said the first lieutenant. "What did he say this time, Guns?"

"Usual brag. Said the one batch of those American destroyers might have managed to squeak across the Atlantic, but the world could be sure no other would ever get there."

The captain turned to me, "How do you take your porridge in America—with sugar or salt?"

"With sugar, usually."

"So do we. Heard you took it the Scotch way. Personally, I could never learn to like it with salt."

"Imagine! Boasting that none of this bunch would get through," persisted the sub. "Best they could hope would be to nip off one or two of us."

"Would you care for cream?" the captain asked me.

[6]

"Thanks, I've just had it."

"Oh, sorry," said the captain.

"What do you think Jerry means, Number 1, planes or U-boats?" asked the sub.

"Bombers, likely," said the first lieutenant meditatively. "Maybe off the Irish coast. Or just before we dock."

"All the same," said the sub, "we'd better sweat our eyeballs for U-boats when we get into the Western Approach."

"What's that?" I asked.

"Oh, 30 West—25, thereabouts. Along in there the U-boats get lively," said the chief engineer officer.

"Have you tested those Brownings, Guns?" asked the captain.

"Port one's all right, sir," said the gunnery officer. "Haven't looked at the starboard one yet. Thought I'd do it this afternoon."

"I should," said the captain. He turned to me. "Are you comfortable in your cabin?" he asked.

"Oh, very."

"Hughes will be your servant. Anything you want, ring for him."

"Thanks," I said, "I won't be needing much."

I have the captain's cabin and he is sleeping on a cot adjoining the wheel and chartroom of the bridge. The scale of comfort for officers on a destroyer approximates that for inmates of the Kansas State Penitentiary, where I was a temporary voluntary guest last summer. They have tiny cabins with two-decker bunks—a washstand empties into a pail—a single cold water faucet. For the six there is a toilet, a single shower—and, of course, the wardroom.

This is a steel box, about 20 by 10 feet square, running across the ship with a dining table screwed to the center of the floor, chairs roped to each other around it for rough weather, and two benches at the end. Here are a battered copy of *Esquire* (standard in all wardrooms of H.M. ships, they tell me), a portable radio which we can't tune in because a U-boat might pick up its dialing squeak, and a set of poker dice to roll for drinks, which are invariably gin and bitters. These are the total recreational facilities of a destroyer.

The officers agree these are much more comfortable than British boats.

"Now take that radiator (Guns points to the brass coil at the side of the wardroom). You'd never find that on one of His Majesty's ships. Got to crawl in your bunk to get really warm."

"No heat at all?"

"Electric heaters, sometimes. Just a coil of wire in front of a copper reflector. But no bloody good. Remember Narvik, Number 1?"

"Do I? Rather!" says the first officer.

"We could come down off the bridge and fairly sit on

the bloody things, but they wouldn't take the chill off our bottoms. And you Americans do your crews rather well, too."

"In what way?"

"Bunks—and real mattresses."

"Don't you have them?"

"Never. Always hammocks in the British Navy, ever since Drake's time. Bunks are much nicer. But our men are used to it."

"Do the men like our bunks?"

"Why, I can't say that they do, now that you mention it. Something new, you know. You see, you're never seasick in a hammock—it swings free of the roll of the ship. And the men complain that sleeping on these mattresses is like trying to sleep on a ruddy lump of jelly—have to hold on with their teeth. Matter of fact, most of 'em have taken the mattress out—chucked 'em down one of the hatches. Afraid we'll have to refit with hammocks when we reach port. Bloody good little ships, though—fast—just what we need, or I'll be surprised. And your people certainly fitted them out—stores, supplies, even binoculars, why, even sheets! In British ships officers have to provide their own bed linen. Can't really thank you people enough, you know."

The signalman comes up to the captain. The captain reads the message.

"Hmm, submarine reported."

"Where?" asks Number 1.

"Six hundred miles away. Only if the Admiralty keeps us on our present course, which they probably will, and if the U-boat stays in the same place, which of course it won't, we'd pass within 200 miles of it about day after tomorrow."

Then the captain steps around to the chart desk, raises the canvas hood which protects it from the weather. Message in his hand, he makes a neat little penciled dot, very precisely, on the chart. Around the dot he draws a ring. Under the ring he writes "U-boat" and then the date. When he goes to the other side of the bridge the two sailors on watch step up quickly and look at the location of that ringed dot which is two days, more or less, ahead of us.

What I don't know about asdics, which are closely guarded naval secrets, would fill several volumes. What I was permitted to learn on this trip can be briefly told. First the word is short for anti-submarine detector and everybody knows the crude type used in the first World War—electrified metal eardrums in the ship's hull, connected with a sound amplifier, which blow up the noise of the submarine propeller.

Our asdics are in a secret room near the bridge. The

door always guarded. I may not enter, but I may legitimately listen outside that closed door. And I may tell you what I think goes on in this asdic room, judging by the sounds which come out of it.

Just inside the closed door, a 12-year-old idiot child is aimlessly rattling tissue paper. In the middle of the room two old men, rather tired, are monotonously playing ping-pong. At the far end, a stern-faced silent middle-aged woman wearing tennis shoes stands over an electric grill frying bacon in a dirty pan. Now when this grim woman picks up a duck egg, cracks the shell and drops the contents into the pan with the bacon—that additional sizzling noise, mingled with the others, means we have contacted a U-boat.

Rereading this, I find I have forgotten one important thing. Just behind the door stands a beautiful blonde girl with cruel slant eyes. In her delicate, well-manicured fingers are tendons of steel and with them she is trying to strangle a police dog, but she never quite succeeds. What this last noise means I have no idea. Possibly the Germans do.

Guns is 40 and half of these years were spent in His Majesty's Navy, in which he has risen from the bottom to officer's stripes. He is an old submarine man, and has a solid, kindly, dependable British face. You know his big four inchers will bark and his depth charges splash out when the time comes. He is naturally neat, but today I notice one discordant note—he is slopping around here in mid-Atlantic with shoe laces untied. But if anyone knows about torpedoes, it will be Guns.

He gives me his easy, friendly smile. "They're nothing to worry about. All depends on what you're used to. And men are different. Now I can't abide to touch a rat or a mouse—even dead—but my wife never gives it a thought."

"But about torpedoes—if we should get one—what do you wear? I mean, if you know you're going to be in the water, do you want to have on a lot of clothes or just a few?"

Guns ponders this. "It really doesn't make any difference. Anyway, there's never that much time. But there's this way to look at it—if you should get picked up, it's nice to have with you the clothes you'll need after they dry out, and not have to borrow some chap's."

"But clothes don't help keep you warm in the water?"

"Not in these waters. I remember one chap we pulled out in the Skagerak—been in there only 15 minutes—I worked over him giving him artificial respiration for half an hour, but it did no good," said Guns, gently and thoughtfully, "I could feel him die in my arms."

So then after a pause I said, "I expect things are pretty grim in a submarine wardroom, not cheerful and kidding, like we are in this one."

Guns shook his head. "Fellows laugh and joke there

too. Count the bumps you get from depth charges. Bet whether the next one will get you or not." He looked only mildly annoyed, as though I had been ignorantly tactless. "Chaps in that service look at it another way. You always figure that if one of 'em's got your number," here he nodded at me gravely, "you'll get it no matter what you do. But if it hasn't, why, you never will. Chaps figure it that way. Fatalistic. Because, you see, if they didn't—" And here Guns seemed unable to finish his sentence.

"Of course," I said.

"But about torpedoes," said Guns, in his mellow friendly voice after a pause, "it's all in getting used to it. Only since you mention clothes, you notice I never wear seaboots like the other chaps on this ship. Apt to drag you down. When I was in submarine service, and we were going into a tight spot, we chaps took to leaving our shoe laces untied. You can kick them off quick. Don't know that it does any real good. Makes a chap feel better."

"They were saying things might get lively when we got into the Western Approach. When do we reach it?"

"I guess you could say we were in it now," said Guns evenly. "Crossed 30 West while you were down in the wardroom at lunch. But it's just a line of a map. It's nothing to think about twice."

"Oh, of course not."

✦

"This evening just about sunset we should arrive at our first destination, a secret penciled dot on a chart of the lead-gray Atlantic, far from any shore. There London will radio to us what port to come to. Maybe we will skirt the south of Ireland, a familiar channel known to all tourists. But maybe it will be around Ulster and in through the North Channel.

"And what is this North Channel like?"

"Nasty little spot sometimes," explains the first lieutenant, shaking his head. "Usually two or three U-boats hanging about. Lots of little islands and bays there— they slink out and crack at shipping. Of course, it's thick with our patrols, too. Sometimes Jerry sends out a squadron of Heinkels just for variety. Got to sweat your eyeballs in the North Channel."

The signalman comes in from the bridge, rain dripping from his rubber cape. The captain reads the message, quickly looks up.

"Ship just torpedoed 300 miles back," he says gravely. "Asks any vessel in the vicinity to come to her aid at once."

"Jerry must have been a day too late," says the sub, "if he was looking for us. Do you think we'll be sent back?"

"Doubt it," said the captain. "Others probably much closer. That would add many miles to our trip, and not

[14]

leave us enough oil to spare. Probably send someone else. Maybe a plane to spot survivors and drop food."

After a silence we go on with our lunch. The ship is wallowing wildly in 40 degree rolls. Only one plate, plus either a fork or spoon, can be set before each man at one time—he couldn't hold onto more. Butter, salt, pepper, sugar or cream handed to him as he calls for them, immediately taken away. Yet stray spoons and knives continually scoot wildly across the oilcloth-covered table.

Big seas, splattering over the bridge. There is a terrific din as toothbrushes, ash trays and fountain pens clatter back and forth over the cabin floors with each roll. Living in a destroyer is like keeping house in a concrete mixer, and yet this does not interrupt the immemorial British custom of tea, even though the officers have to wave the cups back and forth like tennis rackets to keep it from spilling.

In the midst of it "Calling the captain" comes a noise through the speaking tube from the bridge. The captain rises, steadies himself by a hand grip. "Yes?"

"Aircraft sighted off the port bow, sir." We all run to the bridge, I first stopping to snatch my life belt. The others already have theirs. There she is—big, black, low —a mile away and another mile high. Is she ours or theirs? No one knows yet, and the gun crews of our anti-aircraft machine guns stand tensely at their stations. Since she sees us and pays no attention, she is obviously ours—disappearing now into the horizon haze—maybe a Sunderland on anti-submarine patrol, swallowed into the mist.

Today we should sight land. We've picked up one message this morning—warning to all ships—an air raid is on over the Irish Sea, in the general direction of which we are heading. Up on deck the brilliant sunlight blazes over great rolling combers which smash on our starboard beam. Presently a convoy looms up ahead of us on its way to the Western World—what might be a couple of plump Canadian Pacific liners, what could be the big new Polish motorship, plus a handful of dirty bobbing freighters with British warships shepherding them. Slowly it dwindles out of sight on the western horizon.

"Object, sir!" calls the lookout. "Starboard bow close in." We lean over to watch a ship's raft swing by. Something still on it. Not a body—maybe a crumpled overcoat or blanket.

"Do you suppose the people were picked up?" asks the Canadian journalist.

"More than likely," says Guns, "if they held on long enough."

"But wouldn't they have hauled in the raft too?"

"Too much to do to muck about with a bloody raft."

The signalman comes running with a message. The captain reads, "Ship giving distress signals. Fifty miles astern of us. Say they're being attacked by enemy aircraft and out of control. Message broke off in the middle."

"Does that mean she's sinking?" asks the Canadian journalist.

"Likely," says the captain.

"Think they'll turn us around, sir?" asks the first lieutenant.

"Probably not," says the captain. "Our oil tanks aren't too full. Might need the reserve for a brush with a U-boat on our way in. If we had full tanks you could bet they'd be turning us back."

Fifteen minutes later, "Aircraft off the port bow, sir!" says the lookout. There it is—a speck, a rising black fly, a crow, growing bigger.

"Better have the men at the guns," says the captain quietly. As the cry, "Action stations!", rings through the ship I race to the cabin for my tin hat, camera, life jacket. The best view will be from the gun-control platform. The first lieutenant is already there.

"We may have a little fun, you know," he says, looking at the approaching plane. "Wait now—no, sorry, think she's one of ours—yes, she is, looks like one of our bombers. Probably going out to have a look for the ship that sent the signal. Chase Jerry away if he's still there."

Now the big bomber swings over us, our gun crews at the

Brownings following him carefully. Now he makes his recognition signal to make sure we don't open fire by mistake. The plane fades off into the western horizon.

"Look down there!" The first officer suddenly points.

"An oar," I said.

"Probably from some lifeboat. You know it's damned lucky we're getting these ships of yours. This sea lane is simply crammed stiff with this bloody muck of wrecks, only because we don't have enough warships to escort 'em."

"Ships astern, sir," calls the lookout. We glance back. Two or three hulls are on the horizon. Then, a few minutes later, "Aircraft ahead, sir." And so there is, but she's obviously British, out patrolling the shipping. We watch her drop over the horizon.

"Ships astern gaining on us, sir," calls the lookout. He is clearly nervous. The hulls are on the horizon. Much larger now—must be making all of thirty knots. "Don't mind them, we see them," first lieutenant says impatiently to the lookout and then, to me, "If they'd been enemy they'd have opened fire long ago. These new recruits get windy —as who wouldn't being chucked into a ship for the first time in your life! Most of 'em had never been to sea before they came over to bring back these destroyers." He glances at the glowing blue hulls. "They are coming like bloody hell, though. Wonder what's up?"

In another ten minutes we recognize them as the fat

liners and dirty little freighters we passed earlier on their way west. Now they are making full speed back—and one of their guardian warships is missing.

"Must have sent it on ahead to look after the ship in distress, while the convoy makes for safety," explained first officer. And so it turns out because the convoy, after overtaking and passing us, obviously gets a signal that all is clear, for it again turns and steams westward.

Now I go down to the wardroom for lunch—passing the captain who has just finished his, and is returning to the bridge. When I come back up he is scanning the horizon ahead of us with his binoculars.

"Hmm," he says, "object ahead there." Our captain is a very matter-of-fact man. "Might be a barrel end," he continues after a minute. But he keeps on staring at it. "Or it could be an empty raft—probably empty—can't see very well—only we'll be closer to it on the next zigzag."

We swing away from the "object" on the zig, temporarily losing sight of it although the captain never takes his glasses off the horizon, and then back to it on the zag. Here it is again—lifted into the sunlight on a big wave crest for an instant and then dropped out of sight.

"Hmm," says our matter-of-fact captain. As the next wave lifts it he says, "Hmm," a little louder. As a third wave raises it to glint in the sun, he calls, "Oh, First!"

"Yes, sir," says the first lieutenant.

"Alter course, will you? Think that's a raft out there—rather thought I saw a signal from it. We might have a look."

"Yes, sir," says the first officer. The ship's wake boils out in a mighty curve and the "object" swings ahead until it is almost in front of our bow. The captain steps around by the man at the wheel and continues to peer through his glasses. "Hmmm," he says, "five people on it. At least one of 'em's alive." And he continues to stare at the raft as the big pale green combers lift it more plainly into the sun.

And on they come. In another five minutes you can count them with the naked eye—the fantastic splotches of brilliant orange which are their life belts. Their raft is a huge orange doughnut, and within its circle five men are squatting, one of them frantically waving a canvas paddle aloft. A minute more they are abeam, hardly fifty yards away. As we sweep by, they wave frantically and then sink back dejectedly. But we are only maneuvering to put our ship's bulk between the raft and the wind. In another two minutes we have turned and are coming back. Now our engines are off, we drift slowly toward them, now they're just abeam. One fellow paddles frantically until the raft bumps the ship's side. Now our propeller boilingly backwaters, and ropes go writhing down toward their grappling hands—a ship's ladder goes over our side.

But who are they? These staring, bleary-eyed men with salt-drenched blond hair, who sag weakly in the bobbing raft? "Germans!" guesses one of our crew. "We picked some of the blighters up last trip. One of their aircraft come down."

"Nah they aren't!" says another cockney scornfully. "Look at the uniforms, will ye? They're no Jerries—that's our own R.A.F."

And so it is. The water-soaked horizon blue of the R.A.F. under the orange life jackets—orange because it is the color most vividly contrasting with the sea's blue-green. Numb hands are now reaching up for our ropes. It is much too rough to launch a boat.

One of the aviators rises wildly—unsteadily grapples at a rope—is too weak to wrap it around him—topples into the sea. Instantly a sailor goes over our rail, comes up behind the man with the loose rolling head and wild eyes just out of the water, ties the rope under his arms and pushes him to the dangling ship's ladder. But he's too weak to manage the rungs with cold hands and feet, so three sailors pull his sea-chilled body up and over the side. The others, with a little help from our sailors, mount the wooden rungs and reach the solid safety of steel deck, and are half led, half carried down to the cozy warmth of our wardroom.

Lying limp on the table, sprawled on the chairs, they are too weak even to raise their arms as we strip off their wet wool uniforms to be taken to the boiler room to dry. Their sea-water-soaked flesh feels cold and dead, the texture of cold-boiled oysters. Slowly they mumble out the story. Their big bomber on patrol came down in the sea yesterday. They had just sixty seconds after it struck the water to toss their inflatable life raft in the sea and climb in before the plane sunk. That afternoon they drifted out of sight of land in spite of all they could do. All night they slapped and rubbed each other to keep awake, which meant keeping alive. The water seemed warmer than the air. An hour after dawn they sighted a ship, waved frantically, came within a hundred yards. They shouted and screamed at her, she passed without seeing them.

They were getting ready for another night—they'd saved half their flask of brandy, intended to drink it in one big party at midnight—when we sighted them.

No, they don't want food. Just a drink of water and then sleep. So, rubbing them down with hot rough towels, we roll them into thick wool blankets, tuck them into our bunks where they sink immediately into a dreamless, snoreless sleep.

Meanwhile the signalmen have been busy. Our flotilla leader has given us permission to go full speed ahead into the nearest British port. Men who have been 22 hours in the bitter North Atlantic need hospital care at once. So, showing our heels and a long plume of black smoke to the other American destroyers we abandon zigzagging and, heedless of submarines, forge on ahead. Just at dusk we sight the British coastline and presently are nosing our way up a channel into a British port. There are muffled harbor lights, there are the outlines of two airforce ambulances with stretcher crews waiting to take the flyers to a hospital—and here ends the first task of the former American destroyers, a task begun before ever they tied up in a British port.

3 . WHERE IS THE WAR?

THE night train from Scotland down to London is due to arrive at eight in the morning. Instead it pulls in about noon. The British equivalent of a porter explains that planes were over during the night, so speed had to be cut down to twelve miles an hour.

So all during the long morning I have my nose pressed against the windowpane to see traces of war's alarums and excursions. For hours I see just the pretty English countryside. Here and there, trenches and barbed wire against invasion scar a green hillside. Occasionally a glimpse of soldiers drilling. Mostly quiet little villages, meadows dotted with grazing sheep, stone churches with gravestones gray against the fresh grass—the rural England of the picture books, quaint but a little dull and completely untouched by war. Where is the war?

Then factories begin whisking by. Through their huge glass windows, uncracked by bombs, you see men at work. Some roofs are conspicuously streaked with camouflage as though to advertise an essential war industry. But not one of them has a shattered windowpane—much less a bomb crater.

A dozen of these huge untouched factories slide by my train window, and now we are approaching London. The train slows down for the switching yards, and here I begin to see things. First the section hands, leaning on their picks or shovels as the train glides by. It seems queer that their faces should look so English, and not Negro or Mexican or Italian as we would see in the States. Even queerer that most of them should have steel helmets dangling from their belts. Is this the war?

In the solid row of houses which lines the tracks, I see one smashed windowpane. Presently another. Then half a dozen together—with curtains flapping dismally outside the empty frames. But still not a single brick dislodged. Some place near here there must be a bomb crater. Can it be on the other side of the train? Or have they filled it in? Where is this war?

At last we pull into the station. I hand my bags to the porter and, following him toward the taxis, look up at the train-shed roof. Not a pane of the smoke-blackened glass is cracked.

My favorite hotel—I have heard rumors in America that it has collected at least one bomb, but still I give the cab driver this address—is fifteen minutes' ride from the station. I roll down the windows and hang my head out to look for the war. People going about the streets as usual—and suddenly a bombed house. Nothing very dramatic about it—all the wreckage cleared from the sidewalk and no one paying any attention to it—then another. The little twenty-five-foot fronts of London shops whisk by as I ride and in that fifteen minutes I count only five which have been demolished.

If I hadn't learned from the newspapers that there was a war, I would think London was in the throes of a building boom about half the size of New York's construction urge in 1929, and that these five had been pulled down to make way for new ones.

We pass the old double-deck London busses grinding along, jammed as usual with smartly dressed stenographers. Where is the war, and why is it that the British were supposed to be so heroic? My hotel turns out to be untouched. For a few hours (until dusk) you might think that our American picture of bleeding London was the figment of some rewrite desk hack's nightmare.

It's a nice modern concrete hotel—the British call it "American" and it does have a streamlined gadgety air, with plenty of chromium. It has small concrete rooms—plenty of "compartmentation" so desirable if you're to be bombed in it—and to my surprise I find I have no difficulty at all in getting a room. "Yes, sir—show the gentleman up to Number 711." The officers on the boat had hinted it might be so crowded I couldn't get in.

Then I go out, telephone a few friends, get a little business done, and discover that in order to get a picture of London today you must forget most of the scare headlines you have read in the American papers about a great city in its death agony being slowly churned to bits by a hail-storm of screaming bombs.

Because, my friends assure me, statistically you are quite safe in London. The Nazis managed to kill 6,000 people with bombs during the past month—most of them right here in London. But so what? That's only 1,500 a week, which is a negligible rise in the death rate for a city of 6,000,000. You are infinitely safer, living in London, than you would be if you were a Negro infant living in rural Mississippi. Because that death rate gives you an average life expectancy—so far as getting killed by a bomb is concerned—of about 75 years. Later on I was to find many moments when I would gladly change places with that Mississippi Negro infant.

But riding through London by day I kept thinking of New York in the late '20s. Here, as there, you would pass, in a quarter-hour ride, four or five demolished houses. In this same period New York was enlarging its telephone system, installing several new exchanges, and calls were frequently being delayed because they had to be routed through other exchanges. So too here in London because of bomb damage. But New Yorkers were accustomed to the turmoil of growth—streets ripped up for repairs or for the laying of enlarged electric cables, water or gas mains, entire city blocks razed for skyscrapers.

And now back to dinner at my hotel, where I promised I would eat with a Canadian newspaperman staying there —one of several who came over on our flotilla of destroyers.

As I go into my room to wash, I notice a curious thing. My bath is apparently drawn, for the tub is full of cold water. The maid comes in to turn down the beds, so I tell her I'd prefer to have it in the morning instead, and also would she please draw it hot instead of cold.

"Oh, that's not for bathing, sir. It's for shaving and flushing the toilet. You see often during a heavy raid the water mains are hit, and the water cut off. So if we think the night is going to be a bit thick, sir, we always fill the tubs in all the gentlemen's rooms, so's they won't be completely without water."

Now that might be the basis for a nice hysterical little sketch: Here I am, living in this almost decadently modern chrome and plastic streamlined palace, seemingly with all the refinements of the Twentieth Century, and yet at any moment water, the basic prop of civilization and of all life, may vanish. I decide against the hysterical little sketch. Only that streamlined recessed bathtub, half full of water, staring back at me, *is* somehow unsettling.

On the way down to the bar I look into the main lounge salon of the hotel, just on the chance that the Canadian might be there. He isn't, but there in that lounge is the whole story of Europe today, and if it isn't a good story, it is because I cannot tell it.

A room here costs three dollars a day with bath and breakfast, and there is also a good sixty-cent lunch, all of which is very cheap for London. The hotel is eight stories high, and as I have said is built of sweet, lovely concrete, but it is the saddest hotel in the world, which you would never guess from a casual glance into this main lounge salon, so gay with uniforms. Here are Czech colonels and Norwegian university professors and Polish admirals and Dutch artillery officers and cabinet ministers from the Baltic states now occupied by Russia. Here are the "free French" who follow General de Gaulle, and the "free Belgians" who continued fighting after Leopold surrendered. With a sprinkling of sad-eyed Central European Jews, businessmen or intellectuals, sitting silently with their sad-eyed wives.

Here is the Europe of Yesterday, or at least that part of it which could get across the English Channel to the only country still fighting for a free Europe.

They are at this hotel somewhat because it is made of sweet, lovely concrete and mostly because it is the only place in London where you can be respectable on three dollars a day. For these people have little money left and no chance to get more, with the black Hooked-Cross Legions of the Europe of Today stretching from the Bay of

Biscay up the Channel Coast, through the North Sea to where the Arctic Ocean gnaws at the crags of Norway, and down the Rhine and Danube valleys, meeting Asia on the coast of the Black Sea.

But all the Polish admirals and the free French and the Czechs are very sure it will not be long now. Because they are so sure, and because no one can go out of doors in London after nightfall, they sit here in the lounge salon by their demi-tasse cups, busily planning the New Free Europe of Tomorrow. This they see very confidently and clearly, and outline it to each other with their forefingers on the coffee table, and sometimes argue vehemently about its details.

Outside the big naval-size anti-aircraft guns have been booming all evening, but now there is a great, grinding jar, and the hotel shakes a little. The surface of a big mirror at the end of the salon quivers like a pool into which a pebble has been tossed.

Outside, the Dark Europe of Today has struck London a mighty blow from the skies. Everybody in the salon stops talking. Two or three men rise and go to the door, to see how close it was. They go only to the edge of the door but the doorman, whose duty it is to stand outside, tells them that one was less than a quarter of a mile away—but now will they all *please* step back and clear the doorway, so he would have a chance to jump inside if the next one should come closer?

So the democratically elected members of the Norwegian Riksdag, the Baltic Ministers of Foreign Affairs, and the Polish admirals go back to their tables and continue planning confidently the New Free Europe of Tomorrow, while their wives knit, and the big naval-size guns in the park outside, belching steel back into the sky at the Heinkels, jiggle the demi-tasse cups.

The sad-eyed women knit, and sometimes they listen, but the New Free Europe of Tomorrow does not seem so clear nor at all convincing to them. They do not seem to be confident of anything, except that what they are knitting today will soon be badly needed.

The Canadian journalist down in the bar seems to have picked a chatty hawknosed blond English businessman, and after talking a while we all go in to dinner. The hawknosed Englishman says it looks like another hot night. Even in the dining-room we can hear them far over head at about twelve thousand, some of them sounding like far-away muffled vacuum cleaners, others like angry bumble bees. For some reason the drone of planes can penetrate walls while bomb whistles can't. The Canadian, who has never been bombed before, isn't liking it very much. I have been bombed a good many times before and I'm not liking it much better.

The burping of the big guns outside jiggles our coffee—it's somehow irritating. And I'm very tired. Through my head runs that little childhood stanza, "Now I lay me

[31]

down to sleep." Only first, now that we've finished dinner, I shall have a pot of coffee with them in the lounge salon, because if enough is going on in the way of bombs, coffee relaxes you instead of keeping you awake. I step up to my room for a minute to fetch down my last cherished pack of American cigarettes, but the elevator starter tells me the lift isn't operating above the fifth floor—I'll have to walk up the other two.

"Too much going on outside tonight, sir. We don't consider anything safe above the fifth. You go at your own risk."

What in hell can he mean? I puff up the two extra flights and am presently back with the cigarettes.

It is late, and already people are getting fixed for the night. Some are lying with their knees drawn up on the divans. Others, with eyes closed, are leaning back in one chair, with another pulled up for their feet. And all the while that single line, "Now I lay me down to sleep," keeps jingling in my head. What were the other lines of the stanza?

The blond hawknosed Englishman explains that the people getting to sleep on the divans may be hotel guests who have no bedding of their own, for the hotel prohibits guests on the higher floors from taking its blankets or mattresses out of its rooms and down below to safety. You are allowed to bring only a pillow. Or some may be outsiders who have come in off the streets for safety, for no building in London may refuse shelter these days. "Very fine hotel, this," he added.

"Nice and comfortable. Sort of like the *New Yorker,*" said the Canadian.

"Don't mean that," said the hawknosed Englishman. "I mean its construction. Had an architect friend of mine stroll through it last week. Said there was nothing better in London. He punched, thumped and measured all over the place. All steel and thick concrete, he says, particularly the outside walls—yards thick. Where are you sleeping tonight?" he asked the Canadian.

"How about their main shelter—isn't that deep enough?"

The Englishman shook his head. "Shouldn't. My architect chap looked at it. The sides are all right, but you see it's just under the central well of the building, so you have only about two thicknesses of concrete over you. Not enough. Never stop a direct hit. Very bad."

"What about their side shelter—the one under the central lobby?" asked the Canadian.

"Fair, but still a big room. Best to have lots of compartmentation—little rooms, plenty of partitions to stop things flying around, or so this chap said. Think he's right, too. But I'll tell you where he said was best of all, only mind you don't spread it around." Here he leaned toward us. "Just take your mattress into the corridor. Only of course if everybody did it, the corridors would be jammed like the shelter, with people snoring like bloody hell."

"But there don't seem to be many people up on the seventh floor where I am," I said.

"Good God, you're not on the seventh!" said the hawk-nosed Englishman. "Seven's a death trap. All you've got over you is the eighth, and it takes three of even these floors to stop a really big one from above. Go down to the second floor corridor, or better still, the third."

"But why corridors?"

"This architect chap explained it. A direct hit from above could never blast its way down to third. One landing in the street outside, say a really big thousand pounder, might smash its way through the outside rooms of the first floor clear into the corridor, and maybe even as high as the second, but never up to the third. You'd be left overhanging the crater like a bird on a branch. And in a corridor you don't have to worry about glass flying in from your bedroom window, cutting through the blackout curtains like they were soft butter and then mincing you up. Nasty stuff, glass. I've seen slivers blown into plaster, sticking there like knives tossed into a wood plank. Punch into your skull the same way if it happened to be there, and it's annoying having to pluck them out. Corridor's much the best. You'd be safer than back in the States. Of course you do get the noise of the guns, which you can't hear below ground, and yet it's much safer. But don't spread it about, do you mind?"

The Canadian, looking nervous, said he wouldn't.

I said I thought I'd stroll down to have a look at the hotel's main shelter before I decided where I'd sleep.

In the dim light I see that this great underground room was once the hotel's night club. People are sleeping everywhere, even on what was the orchestra platform. Their breathing is a continuous, sad, uneven sigh. They lie there, the free French, and their wives, the Polish admirals and their children, the Central European Jews, the Norwegian Ministers, in brilliant-hued pyjamas and dressing gowns, but somehow it isn't funny. Some families whose homes are back in the dark continent have built for themselves here little homes with chairs for walls, and sleep together within them.

At about six o'clock, when the all-clear siren will sound, the wardens will waken them and they will go back to their rooms for a few final hours of sleep in their beds. I stand there, listening to the sad, uneven sighs of their heavy breathing. Now and then someone mumbles restlessly in his sleep. A man is moaning in regular cadence, mouthing what are at first indistinct words, but each time they are louder and plainer.

"Go away," commands the man in the nightmare, in the flat, fear-frozen voice of a dream. "Go away, go away, go away!" A warden walks softly toward him, a gliding figure in the half gloom, but he does not shake him. For why waken a man out of one nightmare into another? "Now I lay me down to sleep"—it still runs through my head, a tantalizing, half-forgotten echo of many years ago, and then quite suddenly I remember the other lines of that little rhyme from the childhood of the race, as old as the English tongue.

4 . MARGARET: I

I HAD come to England hoping to adopt a child, and this search led me for a while into a curious miniature world of war-waifs and bomb orphans which is open to few wandering journalists.

I find no place here for the long personal story of how I finally located in London the society which does the best job of investigating the backgrounds both of the children available for adoption and of the families who want them. But when I got myself approved (I presented more distinguished character references than J. P. Morgan would require of a head butler) and two children were to be brought in for me to look over, I became panicky. Because what did I know about children? How could I tell a dull child from a potentially bright one who could take a good education? Yet I knew there must be child experts who could, if I could only locate them in this bomb-blasted city. Then I discovered that Anna Freud, daughter of the great professor, was organizing in near-by Hampstead a charity *Rest Center* for children made homeless by the war, either through bombs, death, or the separation of families. There kinks made by the war in their little heads can be straightened out.

Anna Freud turned out to be one of the saints of this world, and that's a word not to be tossed about lightly. She is about forty with pale even features, black hair, and big, serene brown eyes. She always dresses in dull black, long sleeves and high neck, white collar and cuffs.

In Vienna she was recognized as probably the world's leading specialist in the psychology of children, and had gathered around her a considerable group of specialists and students. When she and her father left Vienna after the Nazis moved in, most of these came with her to London and are helping at this charity child clinic in Hampstead. Ostensibly it is to continue their training in the effect of war on the mind of a child. If these gentle women want to believe that what they are doing is only in the interest of cold science, I won't argue. Only when I later watched them hovering over the bewildered kids, lavishing on them good food and warm baths, did I see that tenderness has more to do with it than cold science.

Over the telephone Anna Freud agrees to let me bring the children to the Rest Center from the offices of the Adoption Society near my hotel. They are to stay at least a week at the Rest Center, and after the place and the new faces are no longer strange to them they will be

[38]

given intelligence tests. No shorter time would be fair
to a child.

At the society's offices they tell me the little boy is already there and the other child, a little girl, will arrive
presently. I decided to get better acquainted with the
boy so he would be less nervous on the long ride. They
tell me he's four and a half and his name is John. I picture an "adopted" kid—somewhat pasty and lumpy of
feature, with a cowlick running the wrong way, clothes
which don't fit and a loose stare.

But suddenly there he sits. Quite good-looking. Going
to have a long, handsome British face. Reddish brown
hair. Holding in his hand one of those English schoolboy caps with some kind of emblem embroidered on the
front. Long, British-pink cheeks, with here and there a
freckle, which should blossom out if he gets any summer
sunshine. And clutching to his breast his favorite toy, a
shabby stuffed lamb.

When the society's secretary introduces us he looks at
me, puts out his hand very properly, but doesn't say anything. He doesn't understand any of it and seems afraid.
The secretary explains the foster mother reports that he's
very shy with strangers, but chatters around the house
quite normally.

But why shouldn't he be scared and silent? What can
he think is going on? How can he understand why his
first father and mother never came back? Does he guess I

am an approved parent, looking him over? He stands there, staring at his feet.

Any minute now the foster mother should be here with the three-and-a-half-year-old girl. Her report on this child, the secretary explains, isn't so awfully good. She's attractive looking, with blonde hair and black eyes. But peevish and sulky. Not happy around the house like John. Also she's naughty and won't eat.

I give little Johnny my tin hat to play with—he's fascinated with it, and is putting it on when the door opens and there stands the other child.

Very tiny and fragile. In a little red coat, red leggings and a small peaked pixie hood. Cute? Not now. Not with that small face pinched tight with grief and those big black eyes full of hopeless despair. And why shouldn't they be—because her father, her mother, every thing and person she ever knew has gone. Yet it is such an intense and naked emotion that I am almost embarrassed. Her big black eyes, which do not quite dare to hope any more, rest on me only for an instant and then leave me— I'm only a man and I don't matter—to search devouringly the face of every woman in the room. The secretary of the Society, each of the stenographers at their typewriters—are you she? The burning eyes discard each and move on to the next. It's as simple and primitive as a little spotted calf bawling for its mother, except that all hope is gone from that small pinched face. But the eyes can't help keeping up their burning search. And I'm very glad to be in an adult world where emotions are weaker and properly concealed.

Yet she isn't broken. She isn't whining. And now she does a curious thing. First with one small palm and then the other she brushes one dry burning eye and then the other. A strange gesture.

"I brought the girl too, like they said," says the foster mother who is just behind her. "But I don't know what to make of this little Margaret. So sulky all the time. Won't eat her food, or anything. Not like John." Again Margaret makes, first with one palm and then the other, that curious gesture.

Automatically the children get in the taxi—told that they must—with no backward glance at the foster mother. Margaret crawls into my lap—not as a child does with a parent, but as a frightened animal might back into the safety of a cave, and clutches my finger with her fist. There is no warmth in that tense grip.

John sits contentedly on the seat beside me and gives a childish chuckle—not at anything at all—just laughs because he is alive and I am here and he seems to like me and assumes that I like him. The girl is wild and lost as ever.

Presently we are entering Hampstead. John points through the taxi window and laughs, "A bomb!" I look and so it is. A gaping hole between two houses where once a house had been. Margaret's grief fights with curiosity. "Show me!" she commands, and leans forward to peer. Presently John squeals again. "Another bomb!" This time he's wrong. It's only a vacant lot between two houses. "But it was almost a bomb!" insists John. Now he stands up with his nose against the taxi windowpane, counting the bombed houses. Three minutes later, "A proper bomb!" he proclaims. You're right this time, John —a proper bomb which left only one wall standing.

Hampstead is street after winding street of comfortable brick and timber houses set in small yards, built in the 1880s and 1890s. Their owners must have had incomes of between ten and fifteen thousand dollars a year. Hampstead isn't so fashionable any more, but it still is a solid, only slightly run-down, middle-class neighborhood. Half of these smoky old brick grandeurs are now unoccupied —their owners safe in the country—leaving "for sale" signs in the front yard.

At 13 Wedderburn Road is Anna Freud's Rest Center for bombed-out children. The staff, with much scrubbing, painting and tacking of linoleum, have transformed one of the old mansions into a war-time kindergarten. A dining room with tiny tables and chairs is in the basement next the kitchen. There is a wonderful nursery— blocks, games, dolls, paints, and crayons. There are four bathrooms, each with a long high-sided British bathtub— a peer could stretch out in it and float free, hands folded behind his head. There the children are scrubbed each night. In the basement, partitioned off next the coal cellar and across from the furnace, is the air-raid shelter where the children will sleep. Two tiers of high bunks stretch from cement floor to ceiling for the three- to six-year-olds. At the end is a battery of bomb-proof cradles for babies. Only this isn't ready for use yet. It must be braced with thick six-by-six-inch timbers, strong enough to hold the weight of the three floors and attic above, should all this brick and flooring be blown in on the children. So far, these special timbers haven't been delivered. Thousands of Londoners who should have heeded the government warnings two years ago now clamor for beams to make these basement shelters which are warmer, more comfortable and just as safe as the Anderson shelters in back yards. Ships bringing stout timbers have been sunk and Miss Freud's kindergarten must wait its turn. But delivery is promised for tomorrow and soon the shelter should be ready.

Margaret and John stop in the hall with Hedy, the kindergarten teacher, leaning over them. Hedy Schwarz is young with blue eyes and ash blonde hair, a gentle Viennese. Margaret and John eye her—John curiously, Margaret with piteous intensity. The big black eyes look through and beyond.

Again that eerie gesture, the palm of one little hand and then the other, quickly brushing the dry, burning eyes.

[43]

Hedy turns to me and whispers, "Does she do that often?" I nod.

Hedy leans down to her. "Would you like to cry, Margaret?" Margaret only stares. "Would you like to cry, dear?" Hedy repeats. "If you do, why don't you?" Staring at Hedy to be sure she means it, Margaret's tiny chest begins to heave.

"You—won't—smack—me?" she asks between heaves.

"What, dear?" Hedy does not understand her south country accent. "Don't you want to cry?"

Now the heaves come more violently. "You—won't—smack—me—if—I—beller?"

"Why, Margaret, no. We never spank little girls. If Margaret feels like crying, she can cry."

Her eyes set on Hedy, Margaret opens her mouth wide —she has tiny white teeth and for a British child they are good—and lets her breath out in a long, voluptuous wail. Kneeling, Hedy draws her against her shoulder. "Of course, Margaret can cry." Margaret relaxes into the luxury of long, loud bellows dripping with tears, no longer do the frightened palms force back the tears into the big dry eyes.

Days later, after Hedy has guessed shrewdly and questioned gently, she learns why. Margaret at the beginning of the war had been evacuated from London to live with a foster mother in the country whom she came to adore. Then suddenly (after her real mother had been

[44]

killed) Margaret, for no reason that was explained to her, was taken to still another foster mother. When she grieved for all that she had lost, and asked why she could not go back, she had been smacked. So you must never cry for everything you have loved. You must push the tears back into the eyes.

"Imagine—to punish a child for crying!" storms Hedy Schwarz. "To cry is as natural as to laugh. Surely little children who are to be adopted and change worlds should be let to cry for everything they have lost. It does not mean this child is sulky. It only shows she is intelligent. That might have been the start of an ugly nervous tic. She might have gone with it all her life—long after she had forgotten the real reason for it—striking her eyes with her hands whenever some memory of an old sadness threatened to come up—and never knowing why she did it.

"A very clever child, Margaret. And beautiful, too, you have noticed?"

I confessed that I hadn't.

Hedy opens her eyes wide in reproof. "That hair and those beautiful eyes! And that face like a cameo! And her movements—every gesture so gentle and graceful! You do not see because she is unhappy. How much that is like a man! Wait only a few days until we make her gay."

"John is good-looking too."

[45]

"A handsome boy. But the girl is very clever. Have you not noticed how those big black eyes follow everything? I think she is much cleverer than the boy. We will see."

The door of the north bedroom stands open. And I pause to look on my way out because on the wall are some water colors—not very good ones, not yet quite bad ones, of the canals of Venice. There are footsteps on the stairs and I turn to see Gretchen the cook. She is a plump, cheery woman just under forty, and the other Viennese doctors and nurses in the kindergarten accept her completely as one of them. They help her set the table, she eats and jokes with them, again they help her with the dishes. Gretchen's little ten-year-old boy Hans who sleeps at the Rest Center, is their pet.

"I'm sorry, is this your bedroom?" I ask.

"But do not mind me—I have only come up for a fresh apron. You were looking at the pictures?"

"You did them?"

"They are my husband's," she said proudly. "He painted them on our last holiday in 1932. This was from the window of our pensione—"

"Your husband is an artist?"

"No, he was a doctor."

"He is dead?"

"He is in Germany. He is the father of our Hans. He was forced to divorce me."

[46]

"Forced?"

"You see I am non-Aryan. We had always lived in a village near Vienna. All the people were our friends and I was so busy and happy! And then they came. At first we thought nothing, I was the only non-Aryan in the village and we knew people loved us—they loved me, too —and I loved them, I still love them. What could we do? We talked of everything. My husband said we should leave Germany with little Hans until it was over. When we applied for a passport, they would not let my husband go. He was a doctor, and Germany would need doctors when the war came! Many nights we talked about it, when we saw what they were doing to the schools. We knew nothing was important but to get little Hans away.

"So it was decided Hans and I should go, and my husband would stay behind in the village to earn the money to keep us abroad. Many nights after Hans was asleep we talked about it, before we decided. But after we left came the law which forbade anyone to practice medicine who was married to a Jew.

"So my husband was forced to go to the courts and divorce me, so that he could earn the money to keep us. And yet they try to say such divorces are not forced!"

"Where is your husband now?"

"I do not know. Perhaps still in the village. Perhaps in the army. We cannot write. The money was shut off long ago by another law so now I support Hans with my cooking. But this I know, that, wherever he is, he still loves me. Oh! surely he must! See, here is my husband, this is his picture on the wall."

It was a carefully enlarged snapshot of a handsome, thick-featured man in bathing trunks lolling on a beach, with a sea dimly out-of-focus in the background. It told me nothing.

"He loves us so much! I am so sure! It could not be any other way. Can you not see from the picture how kind he is?"

"Yes," I said slowly, "I can see."

Since my hotel dining room will be closed by the time I fumble my way back to it through the blackout, I ask Hedy if there is a near-by restaurant. She directs me to one just at the foot of the hill near the tube station. It is run, she says, by Viennese refugeees who make a bare living at it. She hopes I will not mind if it is small and cheap, but the food is good.

Most of the customers, I find, are other refugees who make a bare living doing other things but can, now and then, come to the little restaurant to taste simple Viennese cooking and get a tiny spoonful of *schlagober* on top of their coffee.

When I was halfway through my *Wienerschnitzel* a handsome Jewish boy with a lean, intelligent face came in, and was seated opposite me. He was wearing the khaki

[48]

battle dress of a British regiment. One could get soup, a piece of boiled chicken and dessert for about 38 cents. He ordered this, and also some beer.

When I had come in, the sky outside had been flickering with greenish yellow light from some incendiary bombs which had just dropped. Now as we ate I could hear the planes still buzzing overhead. I wondered about the children. Then I asked the Jewish boy what it was like outside now. He said the incendiaries had burned out, but there was a steady reddish glow in one corner of the sky, indicating that one of them had started a fire. He spoke English with a strong accent.

I asked him if he were Polish or Czech, and he answered that he was German, born in Berlin, but that he came to this restaurant because he liked Viennese cooking. He said the town on the coast where his regiment was stationed was very quiet, and that one had to come to London to see the war. He said he had arrived yesterday on a few days' leave and learned that, during the week, five soldiers who were—how do you say in English, comrades?—had been killed. They had been moving debris from a bombing. Three had been killed by a bomb which happened to drop near by. The other two died when a ruined wall crumbled and fell on them.

He said there were many other refugees in his regiment on the coast and that all of them were most impatient at waiting and anxious to fight. But he said he was very sad

[49]

for the refugees in London, like the ones eating in this room, because there were so many of them, and all so anxious to get a place where they could start making homes and earning livings. But, he said, wherever they went, they would never forget the English who had been so kind and so tolerant when it sometimes was not so easy—with so many from all the countries of Europe trying to crowd into this little island. He had traveled much, he said, but never had he met a people as polite and tolerant as the English.

The boy said he was married and had two children and had just received word that permission had been granted for them all to go to New Zealand, and they were very happy about this. I asked him when they would leave.

"I will stay here," he said. "I thanked the authorities and told them I wanted to stay with my English regiment until the end of this war. But my family will leave at once. No matter who wins this war, we would never want to live in Berlin again."

Then he asked me who I thought would win, and I said I thought the English would.

"We must win," he said passionately. "But even if I did not think so, I would still stay with my English regiment. Because if we do not win, no place in the world will be fit to live in—not even New Zealand. So, if it's to be the other kind of world, it does not matter if I live or die, or my children either. So I would rather stay here with my English regiment."

Then we talked about other things, which did not matter so much. And when I stepped out into the blackout, one end of the sky was pink with fire.

5 · WOMEN IN HELMETS

IT'S the familiar voice of Paul Willert on the phone. He's so glad I've come over, and won't I lunch with him and Brenda tomorrow at the Bath Club at one o'clock? No, wait—better have an alternative place. If we can't make the Bath Club, we'll both of us go straight to the Savoy Grill.

"But if the Club isn't convenient, let's make it the Savoy now."

"Oh, the Club's convenient. But we'd better remember the Savoy in case the Club gets bombed overnight. Much safer these days."

So next day I give the cab driver the Club's address, but when we are almost there, he stops. I've got to proceed on foot. Street roped off because of a bomb. But the police will let me through if I explain I have an appointment at the Bath Club.

Just across from the Bath Club and about three doors down the narrow street, a bomb fell about an hour ago. It had made only a small hole in the roof, a large one through the top floor, knocking off most of the plaster, and then had gone on down through three more floors to the basement where it exploded. The blast blew out most of the building's stone front and all its windows, knocking the three lower floors loose from their brick side walls so that they landed in the basement as a flat pile of old lumber, which is now burning.

I stand and watch it. The man next me says about twenty people are mixed up in those burning floors. The fire brigade is there with a steam boiler booster unit to step up the pressure, and this is playing on the flaming old lumber, beneath which are twenty people who were alive an hour ago.

Off to one side are a dozen uniformed women with grim, impassive, brave British faces under their steel hats. They are standing there with their stretchers, beside their ambulance, to carry away whatever may be left of those twenty people after the firemen have smothered enough of the blaze so the rescue squad can go in. Some of the women in the steel hats are young, most are middle-aged, but all have pink and white British complexions. Clearly they have waited like this many times.

The little man beside me explains he owns the grocer's shop just across the street. Its windows are blown out, and the soles of our shoes crunch on the glass splinters which lie on the pavement. Most of his vegetables are rolling about on the sidewalk, but he's too excited to notice.

[53]

"About an hour ago, it was," he says to anyone who will listen; "I didn't even 'ear the bomb whistle. Just a big crash. I was in me shop and it knocked me flat!" Here he gives a loud hysterical laugh. "W'en I gets up, I can't see or 'ear nothin' for a minute—only this terrible pain in me 'ead. Says I to meself, 'I've been 'it!'" He laughs loudly again. "So I feels meself all over." Here he shows us, slapping the top of his head, his sides and legs. "I thought sure I'd been 'it!" and again he laughs loudly.

But now it is one o'clock so I go into the Bath Club, where Paul and Brenda are waiting. I'm glad to see them, only they both look very drawn. I keep thinking about the twenty people just across the street and three doors down, and the women in the steel helmets waiting. But we don't talk about them.

Paul says he can recommend the Bath Club's dry sherry. So we all have it. Then we order shoulder of mutton, cabbage, boiled potatoes and apple tart. It's very good, only somehow I feel a little sick. The twenty people whom we don't talk about are so near. They ask me for news of people we both know in America, I tell them and they listen, but I can see they haven't thought particularly about these people for some time. They are both much more grave than when I last saw them in America before the war. They ask me if I enjoyed my trip over from America, and if I was comfortable in my hotel. I said I had and I was. They are glad to see me, but very grave and so polite that it is at least half an hour before they ask me, very casually, what I think America will do about the war.

But when I try to tell them, I find I cannot explain at all clearly what I think America will eventually do about the war. I want to say that we will do a lot, and soon, because of those twenty people outside and three doors down under the flaming beams. Only will we really do much and will it be done soon? In trying to explain I suddenly become very sick and have to leave the table. When I come back I say maybe I'd better not have any more lunch. The Willerts are tactful about this and we talk about other things for a while.

Presently Paul has to get back to his desk in the Foreign Office. As we leave the Club the firemen are just rolling up their hose to leave the bombed building down the street, and the rescue squad are climbing over the charred smoldering beams trying to raise them with gloved hands or crowbars. The impassive, thin-faced, brave Englishwomen in steel helmets are still waiting beside the stretchers for whatever will be brought out.

Brenda, glancing at their uniforms, says they are attached to the same near-by hospital at which she works all of every night as a volunteer nurse.

Then Paul offers to drop me off at my hotel from his taxi.

6. I AM BLOWN UP

LAST night I spent a few hours in my bed for a change, from three o'clock until eight-thirty, when I was wakened by the waiter with my breakfast tray. Somehow it typifies this cockeyed world, sleeping on the hall floor and then having your breakfast luxuriously in bed.

For the past few days I've been using my room only to dress, shave and typewrite in. There is no night life in London now, so I usually go to my room and write my article for the day. My typewriter is just by the window— the blackout curtain is drawn, so I sit there typing away and listening for whistles and buzzes. No one bothers when the sirens first scream. This only means that the observers out on the Thames estuary have signaled to us that they're on their way in, and it will usually be ten or twelve minutes before you hear the first buz-z-z very high—much less noise than an American two-motor commercial Douglas makes, flying over La Guardia field at 8,000.

Typing away, one tiny segment of my brain keeps

track of the buz-z-z-z while the rest of it is occupied with prose style. If the buz-z-z-z trains off to the northeast, I forget it. But if it circles and starts coming back over-head, then I get a little tense, and listen closely, but not so tense I can't keep on writing. If it gets just overhead, then, if I hear the beginning of a whistle, I jump from my chair, skip across the room into my bathroom, which has no windows, and wait there until I hear the Bump! which means the bomb has landed. Usually the wait is only two or three seconds. The whole business has be-come so automatic that I'm back in my chair finishing my typewritten sentence about ten seconds after I left it. I do this on an average of half a dozen times during the evening.

The point about the bathroom is that it has no win-dows, so if a bomb happened to land in the street just out-side, I wouldn't be picking glass splinters out of my hair, pushed there by the blast.

Apparently everybody in the hotel follows the same routine. I didn't realize this until last night, when along came a particularly sharp whistle and a loud bump and, about twenty seconds later, toilets all over my side of the hotel started flushing—I could hear the water hissing in-termittently in the water pipes as valves turned on and off.

It would seem that they all rush into their bathrooms and then, when danger is past, so long as they're already in there, they use them. Every near-by bomb is followed by an average of fifteen toilet-hisses. The man in the room on my right is usually first. Within seventeen seconds of the whistle of every near-by bomb, he always salutes Air Marshal Goering with his plumbing.

The morning papers on my breakfast tray say last night was London's hottest so far, so I don't feel apologetic about sleeping in my corridor. You can't get much real rest in bed. You undress and climb in and start to drop off, when you hear the buz-z-z-z of a Heinkel. Maybe you don't open your eyes, but you listen to make sure that it isn't coming straight over. Half an hour later you rouse yourself from real sleep into a light doze because you hear another one. If it comes right overhead, maybe you are too lazy to get out of bed but you wake up enough to bundle the blankets and pillows around your neck, so that if one drops the glass won't cut your throat. And so it goes—dozing but no real sleep, until I get mad, pile out of bed, blow up my inflatable mattress and lay it in the corridor just outside my door, along with my tin hat and flashlight which are nice to have near in case they did smack the hotel and put all the lights out.

I have just been blown up. Not very high—only about half an inch, for the bottom of this bomb's crater was 214 feet from my chair. This evening I had dinner with my Canadian journalist and we knew it was going to be hot.

[58]

Even in the dining-room we could hear the far-away vacuum-cleaner-like drone of the planes—it was almost continuous, and by the time dessert came the big naval-type guns outside in the park began wolloping stuff up into the sky, every salvo jiggling our saucers.

So we went into the lounge, only first I went upstairs for my tin hat, flashlight and trench coat, and tucked them under my chair. All useful if I had to go out through the darkness.

Twice during the early evening we stuck our noses outside, walked up to the corner. There we could see the bluish white lightning flashes of the guns which had been rattling our saucers—they would light up every twig in the park across the street. Almost everybody was off the streets except the police. Now and then a straggler would come by, walking fast and sometimes breaking into a run when he heard a whistle which sounded close. The second time a policeman showed us a long aluminum tube which had just clattered down in the gutter. He said it was the stick which had held some incendiaries. Two fires, better than a mile away, were pink patches on the horizon.

I can't say that I heard the explosion, which came just after midnight. We were back in the coffee-room. The Canadian wasn't liking it at all, and was working on his third double Scotch. I wasn't liking it either and had just ordered tomato juice. It's got nothing to do with character. Only that if something is likely to happen, I feel very uneasy if my head is fuzzy. Because maybe I would jump too late or in the wrong direction. Tomato juice during raids is my form of cowardice.

Setting down his empty glass and looking around for the waiter, the Canadian remarked how safe this room looked—almost as safe as the shelter. And I was saying that I didn't think so, because it was probably under the central well of the building—that glass skylight above us might be a fake, but it looked real. At this point the huge steel and concrete frame of the hotel gave a sudden, nervous jump, like a ticklish high-school girl. It lifted me about half an inch off my chair. I don't remember much noise, but half a second later glass splinters from the skylight above were tinkling down on our table. It was a very beautiful little Sheraton table with clean graceful lines and, I think, authentic.

"Now there's my point," I said to the Canadian journalist. "It *was* a real skylight." Only then I noticed that the Canadian journalist had disappeared. Or rather most of him had. All I could see was the seat of his pants, stretched rather tautly, while he was down on his knees trying to crawl under our fragile but authentic Sheraton table.

I look around the room. The lights are still on, but they glimmer dully through a curious yellow fog. This is dust which the shock of the explosion has jarred from corners in the plaster ceiling ornaments and the tops of chandeliers. Nothing like a bomb to show up sloppy housekeeping. Only the story is outside. I drag my trench coat and tin hat from under the chair and hustle into them, running to the door, fastening my flashlight onto my belt. It's a sweet little job I bought in Stockholm last year, copied from the German military model, and you can turn it on and let it shine from your stomach while you use both hands.

Only maybe I won't need it, because the street outside is filled with the glow of leaping flames. The bomb hit squarely in the middle of the intersection at one corner of the hotel and must have lit a smashed gas main. Outside there is a great stillness. Not a chip of concrete has been dislodged from our hotel corner nearest the bomb, although every window on that side has been blown in. But on the opposite corner a six-story building with thin brick walls and wooden floors had just dissolved into rubbish. One wall was left, a ragged outline against the sky, the rest of the rubbish trailed like a sand pile out into the middle of the street, spilling over into the bomb crater —a mixture of crumbled bricks and splintered lumber.

This crater was an interesting little inferno. The bomb had shattered both a gas main and a three-foot water main. The water was rippling like a caldron, the gas coming to the surface in huge bubbles, where the white and blue flames, licking the edge of the water-filled crater, made it look like a huge teacup full of molten steel.

Looking down the four streets from this intersection, the pavements seemed covered with heavy hoarfrost which glistened in the light of the quavering fire. It was a coating of pulverized glass from the empty window frames of the houses on either side. It crackled as I walked. Not another sound. Amazing it should be so still —that all this destruction should have been accomplished in a few seconds, the length of time it took for the highest chimney brick to tumble into the deepest part of the cellar—and then this great silence. Only now there are sounds. Cries and muffled shouts. The people in the blown-out buildings are picking themselves up off the glass-covered floors, and starting to get out. They stumble down the dark stairways out into the street. By the leaping light of the flaming gas, I see their faces and their hair are powdered gray with that dust and crumbled plaster which a bomb will shake down for blocks around. Tiny red rivulets of blood, from minor glass cuts, run down their gray faces.

Already the police are there. Two of them are dragging a screaming, bleeding woman away from the house which has collapsed.

"No, I *won't* go!" she cries. "Not without my 'usband and my little boy what was in the same room as I was!"

The A.R.P. wardens begin to arrive from nowhere, and

[62]

an ambulance—all with steel-helmeted attendants. But now something else arrives—the nasty buz-z-z-z of a Heinkel overhead. Maybe the same one which dropped this bomb. Coming back now to paste us by the leaping light of this gas fire, which makes everything vivid for blocks around. How can the plane help seeing us?

Flames from the edge of that crater are licking the tail end of that pile of splintered lumber which slopes into the hole. It's burning already, but not much—a tubful of water would put it out. Two minutes later a barrel of water would put it out. Ten minutes later, by the time the fire department arrives, it seems as though nothing can stop it. But they unreel the hose and squirt on the blaze. At the other end of the pile a rescue squad is fever-ishly tugging at the timbers. Word spreads around that a little boy is caught under the wreckage. Here comes the plane, back again, almost over us now—the time before it probably was sliding over in a practice run to take aim. What else can they see but us, by the light of these tall leaping flames—police, rescue squad, ambulances, fire de-partment all busy working and then—look out, here it comes!—s—s—s—s-s-S-S-S-SSSS! Of *course* the firemen drop their nozzle and spring to the shelter of the nearest wall. And who am I to criticize, cowering belly down in the gutter, trying to make myself as flat as possible, my shoulder blades seeming to stick up in the air as high as a pair of angel wings. But the explosion is several blocks away. Quickly the firemen are back, picking up the hose, not more than five precious seconds lost, but it's not nice out here in that leaping light, having to work on with a Heinkel buzzing just above and knowing it's you they're aiming at.

The streets are empty except for the steel-helmeted workers, and the people with bleeding powdery gray faces stumbling down out of nearby buildings, with coats on over their nightgowns and pyjamas, carrying battered suitcases, hastily packed with their most precious things which they will take with them to the deep shelters for the rest of the night.

A girl in her middle twenties suddenly clutches my arm. "You have a torch," she says. "Oh, please come with me—I must go back up."

She leads the way to a darkened entrance, up a flight of creaking stairs—every timber in this building has been loosened by the bomb—another one landing near would surely send it tumbling. Glass splinters under our feet crunch into the stair carpet. There is a smell of gas, probably a fixture snapped by the jar. Hope no one lights a match. What are we after? I hesitate to ask. Maybe a child. Maybe an old woman too sick to walk who must be carried. "It's on the top floor," the girl explains. We climb three more flights, each one more rickety than the last. I am really afraid now. That loose gas on the bottom floors, this whole structure ready to collapse—I want out of here.

She opens the door of her room. There's the bed she was sleeping in, it's rumpled and still warm, its coverlet and the floor are covered with glass from her window and with plaster jarred down from the ceiling. She opens a closet door, fumbles a minute and pulls out—a rabbit fur coat.

She explains she is a stenographer, and this is the only fur coat she ever owned—almost paid for, and all with her own earned money. "I couldn't leave that behind." But won't I stay and have a glass of sherry? No, thanks. Thanks a lot. Not with a Heinkel buzzing over this teetering building and gas escaping in the bottom two floors.

Back down into the street now, where firemen are still dousing the flaming pile of splinters. The rescue men have been driven back. They stand helplessly on the sidewalk, and they tell me about the little boy. "About twelve he was, a little nipper, pinned under a block of concrete. Only the flames came too close before we could get enough men in to lift the block. When the boy saw how close they were, 'e went off 'is little 'ead, clean daffy. Which was God's mercy. 'E probably didn't know it and couldn't feel it when 'e burned."

The faces of all the men were angry under the tin hats,

[65]

in the light of the flaming gas main. The corner police-man, who had come up, clenched his fist, raised it toward the sky and shook it. "I'd like to get my 'ands on the sods wot done it to the poor little nipper," he said.

7 · MARGARET: II

THE British government doesn't want children in London, most of them have already left, so Anna Freud's Rest Center only cares for those who, for widely differing reasons, haven't yet gone. There is for instance the little three-year-old girl on the upstairs floor who would scream if she saw me. Two weeks ago a bomb struck her home and killed her mother by her side. But she doesn't remember this, she only remembers the airraid warden who lifted the great beam under which she was lightly pinned, and which kept her from serious injury. And because her first glimpse was of this man, she has all men linked in her mind with the terrible noise and crash which took her mother away. In time and with skillful handling this will go, they hope, but now I hear her playing happily on the upstairs floor, where the windows are so high she cannot even see men passing in the street below.

The real center of interest at Anna Freud's is the baby on the second floor. He's only three months old and sleeps most of the time in his bassinet, but when he gets his bottle the other children may tiptoe in, and are lifted up to see. The baby hasn't a name yet because his mother didn't bother to give him any. His mother promised to come back and see him when she left him here, but that was two weeks ago. Nobody knows where she is, and the women of the clinic suspected, from the way she acted, that she would never come back.

"Such a dirty baby he was!" says Hedy indignantly. "I think he had never had even one bath. He was gray all over, and we had almost to boil him to get him clean. It took many days."

But now he is pink and white, gurgles up at us and waves both of his hands, and spits up a foamy bit of his dinner by way of making us welcome.

Then there is little Tommy who is two, and whose father was a sailor on a mine-sweeper in the Thames. His mother wouldn't leave London because there she could see him when he was on shore leave. But Tommy's father's ship was blown up two weeks ago, so now there is no more reason to live in London. His mother has gone to a midland town where she hopes to find work in a war factory. If she does, she will come back for Tommy—meanwhile he stays here.

There are three Canadian girls, aged three, five, and seven, who are really English but were only born in Canada while their father worked there. Now he has just been called up (he's in the artillery) and when they know just where he will finish his training, their mother will try to rent a house in a near-by town. Meanwhile their home has been broken up, and they stay here until they know where they will go next.

The evening routine of the nursery starts with tea, only Americans must read the word as supper. No high chairs are allowed—they make children feel different and embarrass them. They have a tiny table with chairs to scale, while we grownups eat at the big one.

Margaret and John sit side by side. Only tonight they won't eat unless I sit with them. Seeing me across the room isn't close enough. And in between bites they look up, to be sure I am there. It isn't because they need help, because although I cut Margaret's bit of beef sausage, and break John's toast into convenient sizes, they could feed themselves very well. But why should it be me, whom they have never seen before today?

"It is because you are the link," whispers Hedy. "All of us are strange. But you brought them here—you saw and talked to the people they last knew, who talked to the people before that. You connect them with the past. Through you they hold a grip on all the mothers who ever loved them, all the other little children they ever played with, and the toys that had to be left behind— no wonder they watch you between bites. In a few days

[69]

when they know we love them here it will become more normal. You will see."

Of course John always ate, but look at Margaret today —this child who sulked and refused food! Two helpings of oatmeal with sugar and cream, a whole glass of milk, tender beef sausage and toast! Then a whole apple, which I give to her slice by slice, which she gobbles down now that she has been allowed to cry and is safe.

Tea is over. Bibs are untied at the back of their necks and each child neatly folds his own. Then they have baths, but I must go too—I shouldn't leave them so quickly. John can undress himself, all except two of the hardest buttons—such a clever boy! Hedy tells him, how neatly he folds everything he takes off, and reaches up to put each folded garment in a pile on top of his chair. But Margaret, although she knows how to undress herself, doesn't want to. She wants it done for her tonight, and it mustn't be Hedy, it must be me—her link with the past.

"But where's my fwennew?" demands John. And I'm floored.

"He wants his flannel," explains Margaret. "I want a flannel too."

A flannel turns out to be British for a washcloth, and the Rest Center has them, already hanging from little hooks, one labeled John and one labeled Margaret. Even in a kindergarten which will handle scores of children, each individuality is respected.

John is lifted into the tub first because he was first undressed. Then Margaret is lifted into the other end. As her pink bottom hits the water she let out an indignant howl.

"Too hot?"

"There isn't any duckie!" wails Margaret.

"Why isn't there a duckie?" demands John. Miraculously there *was* a duckie—brought out from the linen closet—a celluloid duckie which bobs about with the soap. I learn that a British bath might get along without soap, or towels, washcloths, sponges, or maybe without even water, but if there isn't a duckie it isn't a bath.

Upstairs into cribs side by side, and then a crisis.

"Will you sleep near us?" John demands.

No, Hedy explains, Mr. White must go back to his hotel where he always sleeps. Both children begin to cry.

"I'll come back tomorrow night." But tomorrow is centuries away.

"I want him to keep near us," wails Margaret.

"Couldn't you this one night?" whispers Hedy. "Everything is so strange to them." So it is settled and they make a bed for me against the wall, across from the two cribs. The children quiet down while I strip to my shorts and crawl into bed. Six-thirty isn't my usual bedtime. On

[71]

the night table is an old copy of the *Psychoanalytic Review*—devoted to case histories of young children.

Presently I find myself fascinated. What queer bugs children get in their little heads, and yet how logically the bugs crawl in there! Not because children are stupid. Only because they haven't had time to learn. First things come first. It probably takes as much nerve training to stand upright as it does to learn Italian.

Suddenly an explosion shakes the house. I put down my book and look at my watch. Ten o'clock. Another explosion! The old house trembles. Guns or bombs? No way to know. But close, which ever it was. I don't like this house. Don't like it at all. Brick with high-ceilinged rooms and wooden beams which even a light near-by blast would send crumbling into the basement. I remember my nice concrete hotel. Then I remember these gentle Viennese women who sleep in this death-trap every night because here they can help the children. Another explosion. If I'd slept here before I'd know whether or not these were merely anti-aircraft guns firing from some near-by park or perhaps were bombers. Margaret sits up in bed wide-eyed. John too. Both are looking at me.

Another deep explosive thump and the floor quivers. John laughs gleefully at the big noise, but not Margaret.

"A bombah!" she says.

"Oh no," I say, "it's only our guns, chasing the bombers away." I wish I could be sure.

"It sounds like a bombah," says Margaret. John says nothing. His head sinks back on his pillow. Does he know what a bomber is? Certainly Margaret knows. There are no more explosions and presently Margaret lies back again. But for a long time her eyes are open, watching me from her pillow uneasily. At last she sleeps. Probably it was only guns, firing at some target far on the horizon. I heard no sound of a plane. But sometimes they come gliding in low with their motors cut. At last I too drop off to sleep in the silent house.

For how long I do not know. At first I think the noise may be only a dream. Then all at once I know it isn't. To the north and coming nearer, quite a way off still, but distinct, the desynchronized motors of a Heinkel, droning like a couple of bumble bees. I hear Margaret stir in bed.

Nearer now, but not loud. Coming down to us from twenty thousand. A noise you would never notice at night in America. Only in London, your ears can pick out that muffled hum through walls. Margaret moans in her sleep. Will it pass over us? It sounds that way, unless it alters course. If they meant to drop something on us, they would unload about half a minute before they got

[73]

directly overhead. But then it would take it roughly half a minute to drop from twenty thousand. If it is going to land close, the explosion will come when the sound of the motors is directly above. Margaret moans again. She sits up. No sound from John. So without turning on the light which might wake him, I tiptoe over to her crib. She is sitting up.

"Is it a Germanplane?" It's one word for her.

"Oh no," I whisper. In the darkness I can see her hands are stretched out toward me to be picked up.

"I don't like Germanplanes. Will it go way?" she whispers.

"Oh yes. I think it's one of ours sent to chase the German plane away."

"Will it go soon?" Margaret whispers.

"Very soon." John has not stirred. We can hear his even breathing. Of course the noise isn't loud. Not loud enough to wake you unless you know what it is. It's directly over us now and Margaret's arms are tight around my neck.

"When will it go away?" she asks.

"Very soon," I say evenly. Only I don't feel even. Because if anything is going to happen, it should happen now. Or the next second. Or the one after that. Surely the time is past now, because, by the sound, the plane has passed the zenith. Surely. These women, who live

[74]

in the ramshackle old house which a bomb could smash like a berry crate, could easily move to the safety of some little rural town or even to America, and who would blame them? Only the job to do is here. The noise comes more faintly now, and Margaret relaxes her arms around my neck. I slip her back into her crib.

"Tuck me in," she commands, with eyes closed. John hasn't waked up at all.

Next morning before I leave for work I tell Hedy Schwarz what happened during the night.

"Poor little boy!" she says. I don't understand, and explain that it was the girl who was frightened.

"She is very clever. Even at three and a half she knows enough to be afraid. Because to be afraid or to be sad is not necessarily to be stupid—if there are things which you should fear or should make you grieve. But little John I am afraid will not do well on his intelligence tests. And what a pity it is, because he is such a charming boy, and gives his love so easily and quickly!"

8. THE ROAD
TO THE CROSSES

THE little station wagon belonging to the air ministry at Whitehall was puttering along the smooth macadam road through Kent. The uniformed girl at the wheel was a member of the Woman's Army Air Force. Now and then, without turning around to us, she would point out to the conducting officer next to me some new bomb damage. Maybe a row of cottages whose windows had been broken since last week. Maybe a new crater at a railway crossing, indicating that the Germans had been shooting for the railway bridge.

Whatever she had to say was said easily, but it was never familiar, and she always said "sir." It was all strictly within the boundaries of military discipline. As we were leaving London I had got out a cigarette for myself, and offered one to the conducting officer who thanked me. And then I said:

"Would you care for one, driver?"

"If I have permission." She didn't turn her head.

"Oh yes," said the conducting officer. "It'll be quite all right."

Only then did she take a hand off the wheel to reach back for one.

The WAAFs are nice because they have good steady British nerves, and are serious about the war. I have never seen one of them go female on duty. Out of uniform they can be as coquettish and whimsical as anyone could wish.

We were on our way out to one of the big fighter airfields of that ring which defends London, where the kids go up to beat them back, when they come in over the Channel or up the Thames Estuary. Squadron Leader Melvin Eaton had invited me to come out and visit the squadron of Spitfires which he has been commanding for more than a year, during which time he has got two bullets in him—not counting a couple more which went in one side and out the other—has bailed out twice, and successfully landed two other planes so badly shot up they were hauled away for junk.

I turned around in my seat to look back at London. Kent is a fat, flat farming country like Iowa. On the distant horizon London was only a black streak. Above it was a dotted line of barrage balloons which clearly outlined the big town on the horizon. They looked like a bed of toadstools with long, thin stems.

It made me think of little towns in what later became the dust bowl as they looked twenty years ago. Driving toward one of them, you could first see it about thirty miles away. But you would not see treetops, for that country was even then too dry for trees. First of all you would see not the town's sun-silvered shingle roofs, but what looked like a wide patch of glistening metal sunflowers rising above the level horizon. These were the fan blades of the zinc-plated windmills in every backyard which pumped the household water.

The last war mowed down these glittering patches of zinc sunflowers, for with its wheat money each little prairie town installed a deep municipal well, a high water tank and a water system. But the wheat belt is now the dust bowl. This new war has raised a patch of giant toad-stools towering five thousand feet over London.

"Good, clear morning," said the conducting officer. "If there's any fighting around we should see it plainly. Last time I was out here we could count half a dozen para-chutes coming down at once."

"By the way," I asked, "how high do casualties run in fighter squadrons?"

"Tell you that exactly. Some of the chaps at the ministry have been totting it up unofficially. From the start of the Germans' drive into France, on down through Dun-kirk and the September blitz over London to now, they estimate that a British fighter pilot has had average life expectancy of six months."

I didn't say anything for a minute. Then I asked, "You

mean that the boys we're going out to visit today have six months to live?"

"You could say that. This is a pretty active station, although of course those figures include hundreds of those chaps who are shot down in their first fight."

This checked with something Eaton had said the week before in London.

"Most dangerous time for any chap in fighters is the first time he goes up in a real fight. Certain things about fighting they can't ever teach you in training school. It's not the real thing. If a bloke gets on your tail, what the hell, he's just a pal of yours, and it's only a game of dodging and twisting to throw him off. But when you look around and find a Messerschmitt behind you with a Jerry shooting past your ear, you find you have to learn it all over again. Lots of chaps forget everything they learned. It's really slaughter. Jerry knocks them down like sparrows. When a chap has pulled through his first two or three fights, he knows Jerry's tricks, and he's really pretty safe from then on."

Only of course you weren't very safe. But did Eaton and fellows like him in Spitfires ever stop to think how great were the risks? If they did, you could be sure that fellows like Eaton would not be talking about it.

Yet there was that curious remark Eaton had made about his family. I had just met his pretty wife—a tall, black-haired girl with a pink and white British skin and clear blue eyes, about twenty-five years old. Their baby son is almost a year and a half.

"We were also planning a girl," he was telling me later "—of course we were very sure the next would be a girl. But then we decided against another one. You see, the boy was born before the war."

"But why don't you want a girl?"

"We do very much. Jenifer does still. Only when I got on operational flying I decided it was too big a risk. It will put too big a burden on her. Might, I mean."

After a minute I said, "Does your wife mind your being on operational flying?"

"We talked it all out when the war started. Jenifer understands. Bloody fine girl—plucky, too. I say, let's talk about something else. And I think I'll have a brandy. Waiter!—a couple more brandies, please."

So probably Eaton knew—maybe all of them knew. But did they realize the time was as short as six months?

We had turned off the macadam road down a lane, shaded with foliage yellowing from early autumn. Ahead of us were the great camouflaged hangar buildings.

"I say," said the conducting officer, "what I told you about the six months isn't exactly hush-hush—but I shouldn't mention it here at the station."

"Don't they know it?"

"Don't know that they think much about it. If they

ever do, they can figure their chances better than we can. They see their own friends go down."

"Naturally."

"From now on it may not be so high. After all there won't be another Dunkirk. And we seem to have cured Jerry of daylight raiding. So it may stretch to nine months or a year."

The car pulls up by a camouflaged building, and we are greeted by a flight lieutenant who explains that Eaton is expecting us, but headquarters ordered him to take a couple of flights up on patrol about an hour ago. Should be down any time. Meanwhile, could he do the honors of the station and would we like to look around? It's all the usual thing, he insists—this, the mess hall; this, the cots where the chaps sleep; and then, oh yes, this big room with the long table is where they roll and pack parachutes.

It's in charge of one little red-headed WAAF, and has to be done carefully, too, on that big table—every wrinkle out and every fold just right, like making a baby's bed.

And don't think the chaps don't appreciate a good job well done. Last month someone mentioned the fact that not one of the parachutes packed at this station had ever failed to open full—just hopped out when you yanked the release cord—so all the chaps who had bailed out took up a collection to buy a gold military wrist watch for the little red-headed WAAF, just to show her they appreciated it.

And yet in spite of everything, insists the flight lieutenant, amusing things will happen to chutes. For instance, the devil of an amusing thing happened to him last week. These two Jerries had dived on him and one had showered his petrol tank and set it afire so that he had to bail out. It had been a rather close thing, and he was feeling rather satisfied with himself to be so well out of it, floating gently down, when he felt a curious tickling behind him. Three of his chute cords were dangling. He glanced up, and by George, one corner of the bloody parachute was afire, and he was still about two thousand feet from the ground! Well, not really afire, but smoldering—the way a bit of newspaper will smolder in a widening red ring if you drop a cigarette on it.

The thing that made it so amusing was the carefree way he had felt when he hopped out of his cockpit and then felt that nice tug under his armpits. He'd felt so safely out of it, so comfortable—and now to look up at that bloody smoldering ring, growing wider all the time! It had eaten into about a square yard of the cloth—the rush of air against the smoldering edges made them burn faster and faster, and every second he expected the smoldering silk to break into flame and let him plummet like a rock onto the ground. Of course nothing really happened—he got to the ground before the filthy thing actually broke into flames; matter of fact, he came smack down in a two-foot deep cow pond with plenty of nice mud to break the jar—but still there was no place like the airforce, if you had a sense of humor, because amusing things like that kept happening all the time.

On the way back to headquarters we walked past five Spitfires in a line, their hoods raised and their ground crews on ladders busily overhauling their long black motors.

"We've got a fine ground force here," says the flight lieutenant, "one of the best. You know those chaps feel they practically do the fighting—great rivalry among them, each crew wanting to send its plane up with the motor purring smooth as velvet, all its machine guns feeding properly, every dial accurate and everything shipshape. And when a pilot knocks a Jerry out, that night his ground crew talks about 'that Jerry *we* brought down' —they're sure they do the actual work and the pilot is only their field representative."

At the door we stopped to watch a big air fight high in the northeastern sky. We could not see the planes which were between twenty-five and thirty thousand feet up. But we could make out the thin trailing plumes of steam thin white and pearly in the sun, which were twelve Messerschmitts coming in. At the very tip each strand was thin as a glistening spiderweb—then it widened to a fine thread of gleaming catgut, thus gradually broadened and fluffed out until, five or ten minutes back of its fine point, it was perceptibly a thick fluffy rope of fog.

The attacking twelve Messerschmitts were flying in formation. One British flight was diving to meet them in a slow-moving curve. Occasionally a plane would be visible for an instant, at the end of its white strand, when it turned over in the air and the sun glinted on its wings. The diving curve seemed to move very slowly—about half the speed of the second hand of a watch. It was hard to realize that actually the planes making these spirals were going at 350 miles an hour.

"Is that Eaton and the other chaps?" I asked.

"Wouldn't think so," said the flight lieutenant. "This scramble is just about over the Estuary. Rather think headquarters sent Eaton and the others over toward Dover. By George, here they come now—they're coming in."

A speed of 350 miles an hour is hard to visualize. When you grasp it there is little to compare it to. The first Spitfire roared in over the great field so fast that it seemed like a bat quickly flashing by your eyes in the twilight, before you have time to turn your head. Flying at better than five miles a minute, the Spitfire with a great roar passed over from horizon to horizon and presently roared in again more slowly for a landing. Then another Spitfire, and another, taxiing up toward our hangar. Now the boys are climbing out, still muffled in their helmets and

[84]

flying suits, and striding toward the intelligence officer, who has come out to meet them with his pad and pencil ready.

As squadron leader and commander of the field, Eaton reports to the intelligence officer first, and I think again how much he looks like Leslie Howard. He has taken off his helmet and it's the same curly hair, the same long, delicately molded and sensitive profile, the same restraint in the way he talks. As the other boys tell their versions of the morning, and the intelligence officer's pencil jigs over the pad, Eaton steps over to me.

"Nothing happened," he explains; "just the usual patrol. Go up to thirty thousand, then back and forth until headquarters telephones up it's time for you to come down and they send up two other flights to take your place. We sighted only two Jerries—Dorniers they looked like—coming over from around Calais. As soon as they saw us they turned back. Bloody fine view though this morning—one of the best, out of the top drawer—London and everything."

"What does London look like from the air?"

"Depends on where you are. From eight thousand feet you have the whole thing spread out before you, and all clear—streets and everything. Make a wonderful target—you can pick out all the parks and squares and railway stations. But of course on a clear day like this, Jerry would never dare come that low—he'd be only sending over

[85]

stray Messerschmitts each with a single 250-pound bomb slung underneath, flying at 25,000 or 30,000. Of course they're only a minor nuisance—the extra weight drags them back, and when we catch up with them they have to jettison their bomb wherever they are, in order to run away from us. Now and then one or two sneak through—you've heard them bumping around London occasionally in the daytime."

I nodded.

"Of course at 30,000 there's no question of aimed bombing. London shrivels up to a grayish brown scar no bigger than a book dropped at your feet. You can see the Thames Estuary and the Channel and, beyond, the coast of France, all of them looking exactly as they do on the map. Only at 30,000 the villages disappear; they're too tiny to see—only fair-sized towns are left. Roads vanish, except for the new four-lane concrete highways—now and then the sunlight will catch one of these just right, and it will glint at you like a cobweb and then disappear. By the way, it was bloody cold up there this morning—step over and take a look at my windscreen."

We walked over to the plane and he gave me a hand up onto the wing. The thick composition glass windscreen over the front of the cockpit seemed to have been sandblasted, but when I scratched it with my fingernail it was only hard ice frost.

"You see a few minutes ago I was six miles up and the

temperature there is about ten or twenty below zero. So on the way down, the minute I strike the warm layer of air near the earth—yes, I know it doesn't feel very warm to you today, but relatively it is—the glass of that windscreen is still so bloody cold that moisture condenses on it and freezes, so thick I sometimes have to raise up in my seat to see the ground when I come in on a landing. But now let's pop in the mess for a bite of lunch. The chaps'll all be glad to see you again—after you left last time they agreed you were a good type."

"But what's a type?"

"Airforce talk. You Americans would say guy or chap. Comes from the typing we get when we join up. Each man gets tests which decide whether he's bomber type, fighter type, ground type, or whatever he is."

"What's the bomber type?"

"Oh, steady, well-intentioned, plodding chaps, good at math, navigators, always think twice—we think they're a bit slow. Of course Whitehall's right about it—you've got to have a steady, level-headed chap in charge when you send him up with a crew of four and a bomber worth a quarter million of your American dollars. Can't afford to let fools kill themselves in planes like that. Still, we fighters think the bomber type's a bit on the dull side."

"Then what's the fighter type?"

"Just the opposite—crazy."

"Oh, come along."

"No. No—I'm right, really crazy. Got to be crazy in fighters. Can't ever stop to think. Got to act instead of think in fighters. If you stop to think at 350 miles an hour it's too late and Jerry's got you."

As we walked toward the mess I began to understand what he meant. I remembered my first meal with these boys. They were friendly enough, but they had come at me with abrupt, blunt questions—had sometimes slashed into the middle of my reply with a flat contradiction—not rudely, but just as impulsively as any one of them might have seized a chance to come roaring down on one wing, across the tail of a Messerschmitt to give it a burst of fire.

It was the same at the lunch today. The boys were so alert that they seemed to have only bundles of quivering nerves under their skins, rather than flesh and fat.

"What the devil do you Americans mean, building your own fighters? Why don't you copy ours?"

"Our designers think some of their own ideas are pretty good."

The boy waved this aside with a gesture which was impatient yet still friendly.

"Maybe. But how can anyone know until they've taken them up in a scramble? We found out as soon as the real show started that half the peacetime designing was all bosh. Take that bloody cowling we started with. If Jerry put a cannon shot through your motor and you wanted to bail out, you were supposed to raise your hand over your head, push the cowling forward, crawl out, hop free and pull your chute cord.

"Trouble was, if your plane was falling, spinning around in the air, the wind pressure on that cowling kept pushing it back harder than the poor devil inside could push it forward—so dozens of chaps went smack into the ground, trapped in their cockpits.

"Finally one survived to report that wind pressure was jamming against that cowling so hard he was only just able to ram it open and squeeze out in time for his chute to open. Then they changed the cowling to open by pushing it backward—*with* the wind pressure, instead of *against* it. Your American designers are probably good chaps at paper work—but how the devil can they know what they're doing unless their stuff is being used?"

I didn't answer, partly because the boys were all listening to a little blond pilot, sitting across the table and three places down. He was one of the six who had been on patrol that morning.

"Think he was one of ours," the boy was saying, "pretty sure of it. His chute had opened, and when I saw him he was floating down at about fifteen thousand. I noticed this Jerry doing figure eights about the bloke, giving him a burst of fire every time he passed. I was at about twenty thousand so I dived on the Jerry and chased him away. Then I circled back to have a look at the bloke."

[89]

"Had the Jerry got him?"

"Think so. As he went by me I could see his head hanging over like this—" and the little blond pilot illustrated by letting his own head sink limply down on his tunic, his mouth and eyes half open. "Bloke must have lost his head—pulled his rip cord too soon."

"But," I said, "I thought you were supposed to pull it as soon as you are clear of your plane."

"Not when Jerries are about," explained the flight lieutenant. "You see if you bail out above twenty thousand, it may take you the better part of half an hour to come down, with your chute open. There you float, a wonderful target for any Jerry who wants to come zooming by and give you a burst of fire. What you do instead is let yourself drop free until you're a thousand feet above the ground—it keeps coming at you and getting bigger and bigger—you are usually falling head first by that time, because your feet drag back like a rudder, so there's no danger you won't see the ground in time to pull your cord. There's really plenty of time because a man is relatively light in the air and falls slowly—he doesn't come whistling down as fast as a bomb."

"What does it feel like, falling free?"

"Last time I bailed out, it felt wonderful. The Jerry had put a hole through my gas tank so, before I could wiggle out of the cockpit, I had some bad burns on my cheek and one hand. The cool air whistling over those burns felt so nice I could hardly bear to pull my cord. Only thing that was wrong was, when I kicked loose from the plane, I somehow kicked myself into a spin. Turning over and over like that, I felt a little seasick by the time I was down to about 1,000 feet."

"Do you chaps machine gun German pilots when you see them coming down in parachutes?"

"Why should we? We know they'll never bother us again. If they do make a landing they'll spend the rest of the war in a prison camp. You see, Jerry takes all the risks over England. Two weeks ago I was out in patrol with another chap at about 20,000 and we spotted two squadrons of Heinkel bombers at about fifteen. Above them were at least a dozen Messerschmitt fighters at about 30,000—supposed to be covering those Heinkels.

"Well, this chap and I decided we'd have a go at the Heinkels, so we dived in amongst them, and they all scattered for home. But not one of those Messerschmitts came down for a scramble. They kept right on in formation, pretending they didn't see us. Jerry knows that, fighting over England, we have all the advantage. If he puts a bullet in one of our motors, our chap bails out and next week he's back up in the air with another plane. That's why he machine guns our chaps in parachutes. I suppose if it were the other way around and we were fighting over Germany we'd have to do the same. War, you know."

"But what are the German pilots like?"

[91]

"I met one once," said the Canadian pilot officer who sat across the table. "He wasn't a bad guy. It happened like this—I was about 25,000 and I saw this Messerschmitt cruising along at just under 20,000. I didn't think he'd seen me yet, and so I turned her around and got just between him and the sun. Then I knew he couldn't see me, because of course if he tried to look up toward me the sun would blind him. So then, taking my time, I turned over on one wing and dived on him. I think it was that burst that got his motor; because when I came around into position again he was about three miles away. It was about then that he first saw me, and he made the mistake of trying to circle to get away from me, instead of diving, as he should. You see the Spitfire is a little faster than the Messerschmitt, and can make a sharper turn. That's why, if a Jerry comes up behind, we always go into a big circle with him following us. Because by the end of the third circle you are on his tail, instead of his being on yours, and you can get in a burst of fire.

"Anyway this Jerry made the mistake of circling, so I got in another burst, and I could plainly see black smoke coming out of his engine—that meant I had put a bullet through his radiator and his glycol was leaking—and I knew I really had him now. His motor would get hot and freeze tight up on him, long before he could hope to get back to France. And of course he knows it's all up, too.

"He goes into a dive because that's all he can do, and I follow him down, but this time I keep well behind. You see, the week before I was having a scramble with a Messerschmitt, when suddenly the bloke went into a dive and I had the devil of a time following him down, because he seemed to be doing the most magnificent flying I'd ever seen—wing slides and power swerves and every trick in the bag—it was all I could do to keep on his tail, and try to get in another blast, when all of a sudden, look out! What's that ahead? Why, it's the ground! And I've just got time to yank back on my stick and pull out of my dive in a hairpin curve, as I see that Jerry going E-e-e-e-e-e-e! smack! into the deck, with his motor wide open! You see I'd figured it was my business to keep on his tail, and his business to watch where we were going. It had never occurred to me that it was a corpse that had been doing all that magnificent stunt flying on the way down.

"So this time I keep about five hundred yards behind the Jerry, just in case he might be dead like the one the week before. But he isn't because, about five hundred feet above the ground, he pulls out of those twists and makes a bee-line for our nearest British landing field. It's thirty miles away, but when he gets there he isn't off course by a degree. Must have flown all over this part of the country, because he knew Kent like the palm of his hand.

[93]

All the time I'm following, keeping between him and France. Of course he could never get that far, but he might be tempted to make a break for open water and pancake in the Channel, where he'd have some chance of being picked up by their flying boats.

"So that's the way we came on in the landing field, me behind and a little above him. Only the minute the airdrome ground defenses saw a Messerschmitt coming in to land, they went nuts. Because maybe it was the invasion, or something. Anyway they started a hell of a popping and banging at him and at me too, just in case I was a Jerry flying a captured plane. I saw the Jerry slide his cowling back and put up his hands, hoping maybe they'd quit. I taxied up beside him and we both got out. We could see the ground crew running toward us over the field.

" 'So,' says the Jerry, 'you are the one who have schott me down. Congradulations,' and he gives me his hand. He speaks pretty good English.

" 'Thank you,' I said, 'but think nothing of it. After all, it was only the difference in planes. A Spitfire will turn sharper than a Messerschmitt. No reason why you should take it to heart. Everything you did was great.'

" 'But your work was also good. I should congratulate you on it. For the moment I had forgotten this about the sharper turns.' Then we got to rehashing the scramble, trying to figure out just on what banked turn it was I had popped his glycol, when the ground chaps come panting up, all of them yelling that this Jerry should be searched at once.

"I kind of brushed them away and explained to this Jerry that it was regulations, and he says, 'Oh, but of course,' and starts turning his pockets inside out. The ground chaps would have started grabbing at his stuff if I hadn't shouldered them aside a little, to take charge of it myself. Made it easier for him, giving it to the guy who shot him down, instead of to ground chaps. All he's got is about the same stuff you'd find on any of us—pictures of his wife and kids, and his identity card, and a book of their win-the-war savings stamps.

"Then they start us off toward the hospital, because this Jerry has a hole in his leg, while I find he's nipped me in the fleshy part of the shoulder, just as I was coming out of my second turn ahead of him. It was nothing at all, only then the bullet went on through to my instrument panel and hadn't done it any good wandering around there.

"I noticed a funny thing. Rank must be more important in their airforce than it is in ours, because this Jerry wasn't quite comfortable with me until I'd got my flying suit off. But when he sees I'm a two-striper like he is, and he hasn't been shot down by a guy with less rank, then he relaxes.

"I told the nurses in the hospital to put his bed next to

mine because, after all, it was I who had shot him down. Of course, all the chaps from my squadron came in to visit me, and it was natural that we and this Jerry would talk about all the scrambles we'd been in, trying to figure out if any of them had been the same ones.

"Another funny thing, I guess the Jerry fighters feel about bomber pilots about the same as we do. There was a bomber station near by, and a bunch of bomber pilots heard this Jerry was in there and dropped over to talk with him. He wouldn't open his head to them. But he'd tell any of us fighter chaps anything we wanted to know.

"We talked a lot. He'd been flying for years—in Spain with the Condor Legion, and everywhere. I tried to get him started on all that stuff the Nazis believe in, but he wasn't interested. Didn't seem to care much about it. Guess he just liked the fighting without caring much who it was against. Maybe like some of us. Said he was sorry when the French packed up—they'd been so easy! Said what he would really like to do would be to join up with us chaps and all of us take on the Russians some day.

"He had quite a sense of humor, and one afternoon he got off something really good. An air-raid warning had sounded and a minute later we heard them coming over —a noise like whining through your nose, so it must have been Heinkels. The nurses began tearing around, trying

[96]

to move us down to shelter—afraid they'd paste the hospital.

"Only this Jerry pretended he wasn't. 'Vat are you afraid of?' he says, seeming to get very indignant. 'Ve don't bomb hospitals!'—only then he turns to me with a grin behind his hand and adds, 'I hope!' "

The Canadian pilot had kept us late over luncheon, but now we walked out of the mess hall. "Perhaps you'd like to walk out with me and look over our Ak-Ak defenses," said Eaton. "I'll slip into my flying suit and be with you in a minute."

"Are you going up?"

"Probably not. We've done our ordinary trick at patrol. Only they telephoned over a bit ago, putting our squadron on the fifteen-minute ready."

"I don't follow."

"Just means we've got to keep hanging about near the telephone, not too far from our flying suits, with everything ready to be in the air within fifteen minutes if they need us. If observers sight quite a few Jerrys starting over from France, they would move us up to the 'five-minute ready.' That means we would collect all our gear and stay in the hall, by the telephone, and the ground crew would keep the motors warmed. Then if they really need us, you'll hear the telephone ring, and the chap who answers it will yell 'Scramble' and all of us will dash out, hop in and away we go."

We started across the great field. In the center a little steam roller was puffing back and forth.

"Smoothing down bomb craters," explains Eaton. "Jerry comes over to paste us every now and then. From the air this field looks like a case of smallpox—yellow discs all over the green turf. Nasty things, craters. You see with our high landing speed, even a six-inch indentation might cause a crackup."

"Is that a new one?"

"Oh no. Almost a month old. They chuck dirt in them and roll them smooth, but after every rain the new dirt settles again, so they must chuck in a bit more and roll again. Sometimes have to do it four or five times."

"Something I want to ask, about this business of typing. Do they ever make a mistake? Send a man to fighters who should be somewhere else?"

"There are always mistakes and it's the hardest part of my job. Because the mistakes always begin thinking, it slows them down in the air, and it's my job to catch them early and get them transferred before Jerry shoots them down."

"How can you tell if they're thinking?"

"Lots of things make a chap think. If he gets married, you've got to watch him. Or maybe he's already married and his wife writes him they're going to have a baby. Or if he's been in a couple of tight scrambles close together, has to bail out, and maybe goes to the hospital, perhaps he'll begin to think. All sorts of reasons."

"But how do you know when it begins?"

"If they wrestle and play with each other after mess and throw cushions at each other while we're on the ready, they're all right. But if one of them begins sitting alone, pretending to read, maybe looking out of the window for hours at a stretch, he's the bloke you have to watch. Means he's thinking and maybe his nerve is going.

"Then if some new pilots who have just joined us get into a nasty show during their first few days, or see it happen to their friends, you must watch them. Because our sort of show wants getting used to. I watch for signs in the air, too, as well as on the ground."

"What are the signs in the air?"

"They usually appear two or three days before a crack-up. A bloke whose nerves are going will always be imagining that his motor sounds funny, or that his petrol gauge isn't working and he's running short, asking my permission to go back to the field and have it looked at. You can't always tell if it's the truth or not. Or you may see a bloke who keeps tipping one wing up to cover the edge of the sun."

"What does that mean?"

"Jerry usually dives on us out of the sun, so you can't see him until his bullets begin to spatter. But if you tilt one wing up so that its edge just covers the sun, you could see any Jerries who might be coming down on us. Or a bloke may keep always lagging behind for the same reason. You see, flying in formation, the chaps in the middle can't see much—their view is cut off by the ones on either side. So a bloke who is getting windy will lag back, just to make sure there are no Jerries about. Matter of fact, it's the worst thing he could do, because Jerry always picks off the planes lagging behind formation.

"Of course any chap may start thinking for a while. Take my case. I lost a plane the first week I was assigned to fighters. Managed to land it, but it had to be hauled away for scrap. Next time I went up, I got it rather worse, but managed to bail out and get back with nothing more than a sprained ankle. But the very next time I went up I really did get it. Messerschmitt dived on my tail and simply riddled the plane with bullets—put a few in me. Luckily they were only flesh wounds, although one is in my left leg yet. Left me covered with petrol, too, only for some reason it didn't catch fire.

"When I got out of the hospital I don't mind confessing I was windy the next time I went up. I'd lost three planes in a row, each time had been worse than the one before, and maybe this fourth time Jerry would finally get me. If we'd met any that day I'm sure they would have, because if a chap is even a little frightened, it slows his reactions. That day we were flying out over Folkestone and

[100]

suddenly I heard a loud rattling which, for a split second, I was sure was a burst of Messerschmitt machine-gun fire coming from behind. Instantly I went into a dive, rolling and twisting to shake him off. About three seconds later I realized that the rattle had only been an unusually loud burst of static, coming in through my wireless headphones. So I climbed back up to my place in patrol formation. The other chaps were very decent— they knew what I'd been through—not one of them mentioned it that evening at mess."

"But when you're sure one of the boys is starting to break, what do you do?"

"Talk to him. Tell him he's done a magnificent job, that everybody in the squadron knows it, that he's earned a good rest, so why won't he let me put his name in for something else for a while—work on the ground or maybe over in bombers. Usually, if I'm right, the chap agrees."

"Do they ever refuse?"

"Sometimes. And then comes the hardest part of my job. Because I must decide if a bloke is really as brave as he hopes he is."

"Are you ever wrong?"

"I was wrong once. Very nice chap he was, about twenty, from Cornwall. Kept insisting he was all right, that he loved fighters, wouldn't think of leaving the other chaps in the squadron. I should have ordered him out. But I couldn't be sure I was right. Yet a bloke whose nerves are going has no business in fighters. He's in much greater danger than a chap who's okay. In a scramble he will either freeze to the controls or do something silly in panic or bravado—one's as bad as the other."

"But what happened to the kid from Cornwall?"

"Jerry got him the very next time he went up on patrol. He really didn't have a chance, and yet he was afraid to admit even to me that his nerves were going. That takes real courage, you know."

We had reached the anti-aircraft gun pit. Looking back across the field, I could see that the pilots were kicking a football around near the hangar. It was hard to believe that those boys had only six months to live. Suddenly I wondered again if Eaton knew it.

The Ak-Ak gun was a sweet little job with a long, slender black muzzle which could send up an astounding number of light shells per minute. It had an intricately delicate sighting apparatus which would make it deadly to anything which came below 5,000. Other types were scattered around the edges of the field. As we walked back to the mess the sun was already low, and the conducting officer, waiting there, said that presently we must be starting back. Only Eaton insisted I come in to the bar for a final glass of sherry against the evening chill of the ride back. Standing at the bar, I said I would agree if this last round could be mine. I argued it was certainly my turn, and why should the mess stand me drinks when I could put my share of the rounds down onto journalistic expense account?

"Wouldn't think of it. Matter of principle. Anyone whom we invite here is our guest—we don't care how big your expense account is."

"Well, tell the chaps to drop in at my hotel the next time they get London leave so I can pay them back."

"I'm up for some leave next Friday week," he smiled, "and I'll take you up on it."

"Let's make it definite. Be sure you give me a ring."

"I will," he said.

Then I fell silent over my sherry. I was thinking how very indefinite any date had to be, when it is made with a man who has only six months to live. Only happily they never thought of this. Didn't have to put it out of their minds because they never let it come in. Yet Eaton was also strangely silent.

"By the way," he finally said, "something you said a minute ago reminds me that I've been wanting to talk to you about something. A way in which maybe a writing chap like you could give us a hand if he cared to."

"What is it?"

"Well, it's this way. We chaps in fighters really don't get much pay. I gather from what you said a minute ago you'd guessed it. By the time we've paid for the uniforms we must buy, mess bills and other deductions, I guess you could say we were fighting for twelve shillings a day—that would be about $3.00 in your money."

"Which isn't a lot."

"Not if you've a wife and family to support. Of course none of us really think of doing this for money. And yet it's hard sometimes, when you get a bit of leave, and can't stand your fair share of the drinks."

"Must be."

"Mind you, we're not complaining. We know it's all the government can afford now. But before this war started, there weren't many jobs in England. Lots of the chaps were pretty discouraged, trying to find something. They knew they had ability, and yet there didn't seem to be anything useful for them to do. So now comes this show, and of course we know we're useful—everybody tells us that."

"Don't see why they shouldn't."

"But the point is when all this is over, will there be anything useful for chaps like us? We could have been useful before, you know. And what's to become of our families? We look around on leave in London, see a lot of commercial types who seem to have plenty of money. Maybe what they're doing is useful, too. Only we know we're useful. We'd like to know that our families will be as well looked after as theirs will be when they are gone. We'd like to feel that the young chaps who manage to come out of this show will have a better chance to be useful in the world than we had, before it began."

"I can see why."

"Blokes out here do lots of thinking in the evening. Some of us don't think so much of England as it used to be. So we've formed an organization. Now don't misunderstand—we're not Bolsheviks or anything like that. We know this show has got to be won first, before anything can be done. Only we want the idea to carry on when it's over."

"What's the organization doing?"

"Oh, nothing now, of course. Ordinarily, most of our chaps think organizations are pretty silly. But we ought to have one, because we are in fighters, to make sure the idea won't be forgotten. Chaps who are now in fighters will tell the new chaps, they will tell the chaps who come after them, and so on, so that the blokes who come out of it at the end will know how we felt about it. Can you see why we need an organization?"

"I can see why."

"So I thought if anything happened to the organization, if the blokes who come later should let it drop—perhaps you writing chaps, after the whole show is over, might remind people of how we felt."

"I understand," I said.

"It's really because of our families and what will happen to them. I say, your car is waiting. Look, I'm terribly sorry to have hung you up with all this."

When I walked into my hotel that night, automatically I looked into the bar to see who might still be about. Because the supper hour had already started, it was almost empty, but near the door my old friend the American Colonel was sitting alone at a table. There was a curious look on his face, and he was staring fixedly at his beer, which he had not touched, although the bubbles were gone from the top. The British have been showing everything he wants to see.

Now he looked up, and with an attempt at a smile, beckoningly invited me to sit down at his table.

"Have you been out today?" I asked.

He has been sitting with his elbows on the table, his head bent forward wearily. Now he raises up. He has the trim, sharp features of so many military men, and yet there is in them the softness of a man who heals rather than fights.

"I have just come from the hospital with the crosses," he said, and his voice was flat and tired.

"A cemetery at a hospital?"

The doctor shook his head. "You couldn't say these men were dead, although most of them will never really live again. A whole ward of them—all fighter pilots, all brave men, every man in the room had the Distinguished

Flying Cross—but all of them finished. Done. Everything over."

"What was the matter?"

"Flying too long without rest. Hundreds of hours without leave. A longer, harder strain than human flesh can take. Now they're burnt out and done with."

"When did it happen?"

"In those weeks of the British retreat out of Belgium, and then over Dunkirk, and during the hardest part of those early raids on London. Weren't enough pilots then, and every man had to do the work of ten. Up in the air, fighting from dawn to dark, down only long enough to fill petrol tanks and back up again, fighting hour after hour, day after day, week after week. Those burnt-out boys who sit staring at the floor in the Hospital of the Crosses are the ones who saved England. If they could have had only a few days' leave during those terrible weeks—to relax, now and then, maybe even forget a little—"

"Couldn't they have had it?"

"Probably. They didn't ask. They could see the situation for themselves. There was no one else who could do it."

"How did they get to the hospital?"

"Sent there. Their officers could see their nerves were broken. If they weren't taken out quick, the Germans would certainly get a plane as well as a pilot. So they were ordered to the Hospital of the Crosses."

"What can they do for them there?"

"Let them rest. Hope they'll forget. I'd stop in front of one of them and ask, 'What's the matter with you?' 'Nothing,' he'd say, staring at the floor, 'I'm all right.' 'Then why are you here?' I'd ask. And the boy would always say, 'Well, I'm just a quitter, I guess.' They all feel that! Yet they were terribly brave men! Every one of them with a decoration of some kind! The weaklings or the neurotics didn't last ten hours in that kind of fighting! But each one of those boys feels he let his squadron down by coming there. So now they all sit staring at the floor."

"What becomes of them?"

"When they first come to the hospital, if you ask them whether they'd like to go back to flying, they don't raise their eyes. If you ask them the same question a couple of months later, they'll say, 'I'll go if you order me'—still without raising their eyes.

"Eventually some of them do go back to flying. Still more are able to do ground work with the airforce. But something inside has snapped. None of them will really live again. And many of them will never leave the Hospital of the Crosses.

"Of course," he went on, "those terrible weeks can never return. But," and here he straightened up, looking at me, "you see one side of war. You see the fighter pilots laughing, playing football on their airdromes, eager to go up for a scramble. These days there are plenty of pilots with rest and leave for each. I know that. But I'm an army doctor, and I see the other side. Don't forget this land has paid a price for its freedom! And don't forget the real heroes! Go down to that hospital, and see those poor boys who really saved England—sitting there now, with shiny medals and pretty ribbons on their tunics, staring vacantly at the floor as the years go by!"

Here the doctor rose, left on the table money for his untasted drink, and walked quickly out of the bar.

9 . RIDING THE FIRE-WAGONS

THE first reporting job I ever did was to hop the hook and ladder wagon of the Emporia, Kansas, fire department one afternoon in 1915 as it rounded the corner of Fifth and Mechanic streets on its way to a burning barn. Here I am again hopping fire-engines, in London at the age of forty. I spent last night out with the London fire brigade. I report at midnight and first they take me to a tower on one of London's highest buildings. After we leave the elevator's last stop and are halfway up the winding stairs, our guide pauses to point his dimmed flashlight at a huge gash in the concrete where a bomb sideswiped the narrow tower.

Anybody killed?

"Not that time," says our guide. "Couple of our chaps asleep on this stairway badly injured in the blast, though. No doubt the Nazis were shooting at us. This tower stands out above everything around here. They've guessed we are using it to spot fires. They've been dropping bombs all around us—you can see the ground pockmarked with craters down below—but they haven't killed one of us yet."

Now we are out on the top, above the darkened city. A deep purple haze dims the buildings' silhouettes. Above us the stars shine clearly. The moon will not rise for an hour. Around the tower's summit runs a narrow walk protected by a ledge. This has been raised by a row of sandbags over which we peer at the distant dome of St. Paul's and the spires of Westminster Abbey. One side of the walk is roofed with corrugated iron. "Wouldn't help against a direct hit," explains our guide, "but it's an umbrella against shell fragments when the stuff gets too thick. You can hear them pattering all around during a barrage. One morning after a hot night our chaps collected half a pint of them."

And then we hear it—a faraway low-pitched buzz from high in the air. As it gets nearer we see little pinpricks of yellow light which are bursts of anti-aircraft shells feeling for it, fifteen, perhaps twenty thousand feet up. But it comes steadily on, that buzz which might be an innocent little vacuum cleaner in the sky, only it isn't.

And then something else—it's all over in three seconds—which begins with a steady, low organ note sounding from the high skies and rises in pitch until all at once it is the high screaming whistle of a railway train plunging down straight at us. I cower against the sandbag wall, the others run for the iron-roofed shelter. Then very suddenly it stops. There is no explosion. Not even a distant dull thud.

"A dud?" I ask.

"From here you almost never hear them land," explains our guide, "unless they're pretty close. That one may have been half a mile away. Better to duck down though, because you never know how close it's coming. If they land in the streets, which they usually do, the vertical walls of the buildings send the sound straight up. The whistling noise is hard on the chaps here because each one seems to be coming right at them. And a really good hit would knock the tower over. Gets their nerves a bit."

"And what do you do here?" I ask.

"Watch for fires," he answered. "Just now there are only five—those red glows on the horizon. We plot the direction of each one and telephone it in. Then when the crew at another post reports it, it can be exactly located where the two lines intersect on the headquarters' map. When an incendiary bomb lands on a roof, it often won't be seen from the street until the fire has made considerable headway; it may not be noticed from the building itself if the people are all in the basement shelter."

From here they take me in a car to an actual "incident." A bomb wrecked two buildings—a fire brigade headquarters and a near-by tenement of cheap flats. The rescue workers are frantically tunneling into the building's basement shelter.

After half an hour's digging through loose brick and propping up fallen timbers, a rescue worker shouts "Hello!" Faintly from deep down under the bricks comes an answering "Hello!" "How many down there?" shouts the rescue worker. "Eleven," calls back a buried voice. To the A.R.P. warden of this block that means one is missing, for he knows a dozen people use this shelter. "Any of you hurt?" "Two hurt a little, but they say they're all right. Better hurry up though."

A waiting ambulance is equipped with a long tube which might be forced down to the trapped people and into which could be poured glucose solution—invaluable for reviving sufferers from shock. But the trapped people, to prove they're all right, start a portable gramophone, and a jaunty dance tune comes faintly up through the debris to cheer the rescue workers.

But this pleasant mood does not last long. When the tunnel is only a few yards from the shelter door one of the diggers says, "Afraid we've got somebody here." He can feel clothing on crushed flesh; he thinks it's a woman. Presently, pulling very gently, he frees the twisted body of the little old lady who lived in the top of the house. To make absolutely sure she's dead, a mirror is put to her bruised lips. The body, bent out of shape by the falling masonry, is put on a stretcher and covered with a sheet.

[113]

Evidently the explosion caught her on her way down to the shelter—the stairways were long and her feet were feeble. Only two yards more and she would have been safe.

Now we go around to the other side, where another rescue party is working frantically at a high pile of debris that was once part of the fire station. A number of firemen were in it when the bomb fell. For a while one could be heard groaning and crying out. The groans stopped about fifteen minutes ago. They are working in the dark, and we fumble through pitch blackness, guided by the sound of clicking bricks. Two sidewalls and three wooden floors have collapsed into a basement, filling it with rubble, somewhere under which are the bodies of the men.

"Couldn't you work faster with more light?" I ask.

"Don't want to bring the raiders back. Of course we rescuers have authority to turn on any amount of light we want, but we seldom use it. Makes people in the neighborhood very bitter. They come and tell us they don't want their children killed by bombers attracted by lights we use getting out dead bodies. Can't say I blame them. If there's a good chance someone's still alive we use the lights anyway. Then they don't object so much."

Almost on hands and knees we crawl over bricks, then under a half-collapsed floor, which shields us from the sky so we can discreetly use our torches. The rescue party is squatting in a ring around a deep crater of broken bricks which they have hollowed out themselves, brick by brick. They scrabble at the bricks with their fingers, toss them back to those behind, who put them into buckets for an endless chain of workers to carry them out. In the middle of the crater is the body they are working to release. The dead man, naked, seems to be sitting upright in a bath of crushed bricks as you would sit in a bathtub of water. The level of the bricks in this bath of death is now down to about the middle of his chest. His head lolls forward loosely. In the light of the electric torches his face and skin are powdered a ghostly gray from the crumbled mortar of the walls.

I go out again over shattered joists and down a barricade of crumbled bricks. "Only one good thing about an old house like this," the fire chief explains. "When a bomb blast spreads the walls and the floors come crashing down, the bricks sink to the bottom and somehow the wood, being lighter, always ends up floating on the top of the mess. That means we're never at a loss for timbers to use for propping if we need 'em to get people out."

They drop me at my hotel at dawn, just as the all clear sirens blow. And I keep thinking of the dead man with the ghostly gray face, lolling in his bath of crumbled bricks.

10. MARGARET: III

WHEN I come back it is not quite time for the children's tea, so I go upstairs to see them in the nursery. More have arrived today, but John and Margaret are side by side on a little bench by a low table, where they are intently finger-painting. They both look up and smile but John, with a squeal of delight, jumps up and, running across the room, grabs me around the knees, proclaims:

"*My* Mr. White!"

And it's so unfair to him, because presently he may find out that I am not his. But it makes me think of that old shopworn simile of the tendrils of a vine. How passionately these little orphans are searching for something to love and trust! It's hard to disengage him back to his table.

The room is busier than a Ford assembly plant, and it is curious to see how happy all these children are at work —how strong an instinct work is. Here a five-year-old girl is stirring make-believe custard in a toy pan, presently to be put into the tiny kindergarten oven to bake. Next her a little boy is building a house of blocks. Beyond, a little blue-eyed child has washed her dolly's clothes and is hanging them out to dry.

The whole room buzzes—no game was ever played more joyously or intently than this rehearsal for life ahead. Safe and prosperous people, bitter at those who do not work, should stand in such a doorway and watch the children. Then they might guess how unhappy are those in whom this deep instinct is later thwarted—who cannot find work which they can do.

On her big sheet of paper Margaret paints curious figures. A man? Perhaps a house? No, she explains, one is a little girl, and the other is her mummy who has gone away.

On John's paper are no sweeping lines or figures. Inch by inch he is painting the whole big sheet, as a painter would cover the side of a house. Patient, plodding, methodical.

"And John is also very good!" praises Hedy. "See, a whole paper painted such a beautiful blue! So soon, now, he will be ready for another sheet!" Then to me, as we walk over by the window, she says, sadly, "Even in their work it shows. The little girl's drawing has imagination —every line is different and tells part of a story. But poor little John can only put one stroke beside another until his sheet is covered. And yet he is such a willing child—so eager to please!"

I say I'm glad the tests aren't to be given for several days, until both children are used to the kindergarten. Maybe when he feels safer, the boy will strike out and be fanciful, too.

Earlier in the afternoon I did a little shopping. Wandering through Selfridge's department store, trying to replace a button torn off my trench coat, I am lured into their toy department by the big sign "Remember Christmas This Year for the Children's Sake"—which incidentally is about the only reason the British will have for celebrating Christmas. So, idiotically, I do my Christmas shopping—a big chartreuse woolly Teddybear for John, and for Margaret a book about a wonderful elephant called Babar, with irresistible French pictures.

They understand that I can't sleep here tonight, but they want me to put them to bed. I am still their link with the past. So after their baths, I read for them half an hour out of the book about Babar. Margaret holds one corner of the book, John the other.

" 'Old my 'and," orders John, and with his other he points to things in the pictures which he wants explained, and looks up at me to laugh at the funny things which Zephyr the Monkey does. A child must feel very secure to laugh as freely as this. But why wouldn't he, with the skillful handling all children get at this kindergarten? But I wish I didn't feel so treacherous.

I put him in his crib, Margaret in hers beside it, move

the cribs close together so John can hold Margaret's hand and she will not be frightened in the night, and tuck them both in—all but their clasped hands. Then (they insist) I leave the door open just a crack so they can see a glimmer of the hall light, put on my trench coat and promise to come back very soon.

11. NIGHT LIFE

TONIGHT I dined at Simpson's and got mixed into a bit of London's gay night life, which is pretty exciting when you consider that it is provided without a cover charge, a paper hat or a tin rattle.

Simpson's has changed only a little. The food is still gorgeous and it was here that I discovered that there really is such a thing as great British cooking. Of course the only thing they can do is boil, but in the boiling of each thing just to the proper degree lies the high art. It's like Chinese music, where everything depends on the modulation of a single note.

They trundle the beef to your table at Simpson's, in a polished wood pushcart as of yore, and hack off the Yorkshire pudding under your nose. The portions are still ample. I had finished this, and was listening to the ancient waiter's explanation of why preserved ginger (it comes from India) and Devonshire cream had to be removed from the menu for the first time in eighty years, when there was a tremendous bang outside. It brought all the diners to their feet but me (I am a little slow in my reactions), and was followed in about three seconds by a second explosion about seven and five-eights times more tremendous—obviously a second bomb from the same stickful. It certainly jarred the room.

I stood up in time to see all of Simpson's dignified clients and august waiters scrambling under the tables for safety in case the ceiling was coming down on us (it seemed quite plausible)—all, that is, except one corpulent client who had just appeared in the door, and the dignified skinny old headwaiter who was just starting to lead him to a table. When the second explosion came, the two had just reached the clear space beyond the entrance, far from any table. So the corpulent client was now down on his knees trying to crawl under the skinny old waiter. He might well have succeeded if the skinny old headwaiter had not been down on his knees, trying to crawl under the corpulent client.

Never in any country have I seen the various social orders mixing with so warm an enthusiasm. When Joe Kennedy says democracy is dead in Great Britain, I can't for the life of me think what he means.

When it became clear that the ceiling beams were not going to come floating down around our ears, everybody got out from under the tables and sat down again. After a further interval, the skinny headwaiter and the fat client crawled out from under each other. The client, being brushed off and towed to his table, ordered sherry, roast Surrey fowl with Bath Chat, cabbage, boiled potatoes and a large tankard of pale ale, as though nothing had happened.

However, I had a suspicion that just possibly something had, so I interrupted my dinner and, after some arguing and flourishing my press pass, got permission to go out into the street from the doorman, who insisted the bomber was still overhead, circling, maybe coming back.

Since earlier in the evening there had been no prospect of heavy raiding I had lazily neglected to wear either my tin hat or my electric torch. I went about two feet in this blackout, as dark as the inside of a cow, when the jagged edge of a concrete block bit me on the shin. When my eyes got used to the dark I could make out other huge chunks of it, littering sidewalk and street for a hundred feet in each direction. I assumed a bomb had torn a crater in the pavement and heaved all this around. (Only next day did I learn that the concrete came from the top of the building I was in: the bomb had struck the roof.) I was just making out the outlines of these concrete chunks, when suddenly a hiss began and grew until it sounded like a Santa Fe freight engine running away backwards downgrade at Raton Pass and about to jump the rails.

I knew very well what this noise was. Feeling very naked without my tin hat I prudently dived, head-first, into what I thought would be the protective shelter of a doorway. It turned out to be the softly curving naked abdomen of a marble cupid, which was part of this doorway's ornaments. I have never cared for the baroque style of architecture.

Just as my forehead struck this marble abdomen there was a flash of light, a tremendous bang and a gust of hurricane wind which sent me rolling in the glass splinters on the sidewalk. I picked myself up in a wavering glare as bright as daylight, for this third bomb, landing just down the block and a bit around the corner, had pierced the pavement and then rudely penetrated the happily unoccupied ladies restroom of the Underground, severing and setting alight three small gas mains.

Presently the fire brigade arrived and had it well in hand. I went back to my sodden Yorkshire pudding while my forehead lump slowly swelled to the size of a duckegg. All in all, it's surprising what a spritely evening you can have in war-time London all without a rattle, a paper hat (or a tin hat) or a cover charge.

12. MARGARET: IV

THE air-raid shelter has been finished and the children (still more have arrived) moved in. It is a small room off the coal cellar, with two tiers of four bunks and just room to walk between them. The huge timbers which support the bunks are much larger than is needed for this; their real function is to brace the ceiling against tons of brick and stone which a bomb might push in on this cellar. Another tier of much smaller bunks, no larger than good-sized drawers, are for babies. Every night the little wriggling procession begins. One by one their nighties are somehow got on them and each, still wriggling, is carried down the three flights of creaking stairs to the air-raid shelter, tucked into a bunk. Their little feet feel to make sure that the hot water bottle is there; it always is. Then the netting at the side of each bunk is hooked into place "so you won't roll out in the night." Each one is kissed by Hedy and tucked in, then real wriggling and giggling begins. They peer through the netting at the ones across the way, at the ones beneath, make faces, shout and scream with laughter.

"Margaret! Rosemary! Get back down under the covers! Hedy tucked you in so nicely!"

It goes on. Tonight Iris cries softly for her mummy. Iris is a good little thing, so she does it softly, into the pillow. All the children try not to cry out loud, because they know this makes all the others think of their mummies and start crying too. Tonight it is Iris. Last night it was Rosemary. The night before it was Isabel, who had just come and not yet learned that it is kinder to the others to cry quietly for mummy.

When the last child is tucked in, Hedy brings out the portable gramophone and plays on it the single old cracked Mother Goose record. The children drink in every word of Mistress Mary quite contrary and her garden, of Humpty Dumpty and his wall, and of the Wondrous Wise Man who jumped into the bramble bush.

Now at last the light in the children's air-raid shelter goes out. Hedy's cot is by the furnace. They can call to her and not be afraid.

I get into my trench coat and tin hat and start back to the hotel, thinking about the thick tough fresh wood of the new-sawn beams which are at last over these children like a basket of human kittens. The only sound in the cellar is the soft breathing, the rise and fall of little chests. Now and then, through the night, the far-away hum of bombers.

[125]

13 . DEATH IN THE DARK

THE big jovial wing commander stood by a school-teacher's desk on a raised dais. In front of him the pilots and crews of twelve Whitley bombers, sixty boys in all, were seated on rows of school benches intently studying the maps as the jovial wing commander talked.

He was very like a bluff and hearty football coach, giving his team a lecture on tactics mixed with a little fight talk before a big game. The sixty young bomber pilots, very serious and intent on the maps, were very like the Yale varsity squad in training quarters.

"Now before we turn to the maps," said the jovial wing commander, picking up a large cardboard box, "I have honors to distribute. A little present from Buckingham Palace," and he pulled from the box a pullover sweater, in airforce blue. "Knitted by the Princess Royal herself," and he held it up. Even at this distance you could see that the little teen-age princess had made her rows tight, even and regular—the sweater was as flawless as though it had been done on a machine. "The last one Her Highness

sent us was awarded, as you will remember, to Perry. It
has been decided that this one will be given to Pilot Officer Blake, for reasons which you all know. Here, Blake
—a sweater from the very royal needles of her very Royal
Highness—catch!" And he tossed it through the air.

Pilot Officer Blake who caught it turns out to be a
hawk-faced youngster of about 21. He is blushing crimson under the grins of the other fifty-nine pilots.

But now the big jovial wing commander on the school-
master's dais turned suddenly grave. "You should each of
you have two maps in front of you—first open the big
one." There was an obedient rustle of paper. "Tonight's
objective will be the town of T——, and the primary target is the aircraft factory outside of it. You can judge its
importance when I tell you that we have information
from Intelligence that this works is turning out ten
enemy bombers a day.

"Your course is as you see it on your big maps. You will
proceed up the Rhine to the city of B——. All of you
know it, and I'm particularly sure that Appleby will remember it." The bomber pilots responded with a quick
chuckle. Appleby grinned sheepishly in the second row.

"In passing over B—— I would recommend considerable altitude. We are informed that there are new con-
centrations of anti-aircraft guns here, and the muck will
be thicker than usual. Leaving B—— you will continue

[127]

on up the Rhine until you get to the second bend, at the top of which, as you all remember, is the town of D——.

"And just to refresh your memories, although you all should know it by heart, there are five bridges over the Rhine between the city of B—— and the town of D——, and you should have no trouble counting them in the moonlight tonight. Remember, the sixth bridge is at D—— where you alter course, leave the Rhine, and you will now note the following landmarks. First, you will pass over the forest of N—— which, because it is pine, should look unusually dark this time of year. Just beyond this look sharp for the two lakes—you should be able to see them clearly in the moonlight and, if you are on course, the bigger one—you'll notice it's almost a perfect triangle on the map—should be on your right. And while you are still in sight of these lakes you should pick up the big four-lane autobahn—they've tried to camouflage it but you'll have no trouble making it out if you look sharp—and you follow this right on in to T——. You should see its cathedral spire about thirty-five minutes after you leave the triangular-shaped lake.

"Now pick up the little maps."

There is an obedient rustle of papers in the big room. The young faces are very intent. They look so much like a serious football squad drinking in a final lecture on tactics from their coach on the eve of the big Thanksgiving game, that it is hard to realize that this particular team of twelve bomber crews is going out this evening to play against death in the dark.

"Now here," said the jovial wing commander, only he was now as serious as the young faces bent over the little maps, "you have the target area of your primary target. In the center of the town of T——, and down below the autobahn which brings you in. The target itself is just two miles due north of T—— and you will identify it by the fact that it is fifteen long rectangular buildings, grouped very close together. Be sure not to confuse it with that little village due east of T——; it's only a farming community. When you are sure you are over target, I think you'll find that you can come in fairly low to release your load. Of course there may be some anti-aircraft activity, but since this particular target has never been bombed before, there won't be much, and it probably won't be so well handled as what you are accustomed to over the Rhine or the Ruhr." The boys all grin.

"Now as for timing. You leave at five o'clock this evening. By nine-thirty you should be over target. Now for any of you who, by that time, find you are off course and haven't located it, I am giving you the following two secondary targets—turn back to the big maps now. These targets you all know very well. They are the goods yards at H—— and the docks at K——. Now we'll hear from Met," concluded the jovial wing commander, and he sat down.

[129]

Met turns out to be a little man in civilian tweeds, who rises from this sea of airforce blue. He's the meteorological expert and tells the sixty bomber pilots what the prevailing winds will probably be, and at what altitudes they may expect clouds. A bank which is forming in the lee of the Swiss Alps may be drifting down the Rhine valley after midnight. A low fog layer is coming up the Danube, has passed Budapest and is approaching Vienna, but due to mountain barriers it isn't likely to move into the target area before morning. The presumption is for the light of a full moon which will reveal Rhine bridges, forests, lakes and autobahnen on the way to the target, and should provide fair visibility most of the way back.

So now are there any questions, asks the jovial wing commander. There are a few, and quickly answered. Well, then, that's all, except that they all should be back on the field by two o'clock, except for Smothers, who with his usual speed should have contacted target and returned by midnight. It's some private joke which only pilots at this station know, and they all roar with laughter as they rise to file out of this classroom, where death in the dark has been studied so diligently. In the crowd by the door I catch a glimpse of the hawk-faced youngster, still grinning at the mild joshing of the others, and with his new horizon-blue sweater, knitted by the very royal needles of the little Princess Royal, rolled into a cylinder and tucked carefully under his arm.

[130]

Then to the mess hall for tea at long tables—it might be the student union dining-hall in any American state university. The meal is a substantial British one without frills: big slabs of boiled beef, potatoes and cabbage, thick slices of bread with unlimited quantities of yellow butter. These boys who will spend the night in the dark far out over Germany will be well fed. And as they finish the inevitable British bread-pudding with custard sauce, and gulp down the last of several mugs of tea with sugar and milk, there is a roaring of motors outside. Trucks have arrived to take them to the planes. The boys who are going out tonight sit at tables apart in one end of the room. They aren't talking much. They don't look scared, only grave and intent. As they finish, one by one they rise and go off to the dormitory, presently to emerge with their flying suits under their arms, then to scramble over the tail gate into the big grim camouflaged military trucks.

It is four-thirty now—only half an hour until take-off. The twelve trucks—each one carrying the crew of a bomber—move off in a line to the waiting planes.

In the light airforce staff car, we follow this line of tumbrils. We pass the giant Whitleys carefully pegged down among the huge oaks and artificial camouflage which border the field, making them invisible from a distance of a hundred yards.

Each time we pass a Whitley, peeping grimly out at

us from among the trees, a tumbril loaded with five youngsters turns off and stops. Finally our staff car, following the last truck, turns off and parks at a respectful distance from the big plane. We get out as the boys themselves are hopping over the sides of the truck. Now they are struggling into their flying suits and helmets—looking more than ever like the backfield of the Yale varsity squad. And among the five a face is familiar—it must be, it is—the hawk-faced kid, because just before he sticks his arms into the sleeves of his flying suit I catch a glimpse of that new horizon-blue sweater. But now the conducting officer asks me if I'd like to look over a Whitley before the boys get in. The port motor is already warming up. A tiny ladder leads up to a small trap door in the plane's belly, just back of its nose. The Whitley itself is a huge camouflaged dragon-fly—enormous wings supporting a thin pencil-like body on the end of which, between the two tail flanges, is what seems to be a glassed-in, knob-like turret crowded with machinery. It is the mechanism of a machine gun, for this is the lonely roosting place of the tail gunner. But now we climb the tiny ladder, up through the trap door, into the ship's slender belly, emerging into a confused maze of aluminum rods, gears and mysterious mechanisms. Up there by the pilot's seat is the instrument panel—a baffling array of dials and gauges. Down below is the bomb-sight and close at hand the bomb release levers. That bomb-sight will in a few hours be focused on a group of factory buildings several miles below and many hundreds of miles deep in the Third Reich. I look through it now, and see only the close-clipped grass of this landing field, ten feet below.

Looking back down the long tunnel of this dragon-fly's body, I catch a glimpse of light coming from the tail gunner's turret, make out the machine-gun belts which feed into his guns. But the whole interior of this insect's belly writhes and squirms with fragile aluminum machinery which it would take me weeks to understand, whereas I have only minutes, for another roar tells us that they are warming the starboard motor, so we climb down through the trap door and out.

But just a minute—the young pilot wonders if I'd like to look at the bombs. In the very bottom of the dragon-fly's belly, he opens what might be a pair of cupboard doors and there they are—huge, stubby 500-pounders poised in their racks, complete even to tail flanges—each one as thick as my body. Night after night I have heard the long whistles and dull cr-r-r-rumps as German 500-pounders came whistling down on London. I look long and curiously at these stubby stingers of this giant dragon-fly which, in a few hours, will come whistling down in the darkness onto Hitler's Third Reich. This is their night to howl. Thank God they'll do their screaming many hundreds of miles away from my hotel.

But here comes the bomber's crew, and the conducting officer introduces me before they climb up the tiny ladder. The five fresh young faces framed in the leather helmets might be the backfield of the Yale varsity, as the boys come out of the locker room onto the field for the big game. Introductions are in shouts above the roaring motors, as we stand under the huge wing.

Last to come up is the hawk-faced kid. His flying suit is zipped up to the neck, his parachute in place, but his helmet is still in his hand.

"I saw you get the sweater."

"Oh, that," says the kid, and begins blushing.

"What did you do to get it?"

"Nothing really. Guess they just gave it to me."

"It was like this," said the pilot with a grin, and then began to chant, with mock-heroic intensity, that old air-force wheeze which every flyer recites when a civilian asks of some exploit in the air: "There he was, flying 350 miles per hour upside down and backwards at thirty thousand, with an empty petrol tank and no parachute, when suddenly he looks up to see two Messerschmitts diving on his tail and what do you think he did then?"

"Perhaps then he gets the sweater," suggests the navigator in a bellow over the motor's roar.

"Are you wearing it now?"

"Is he! Rather!" says the pilot.

"What is your post on this plane?"

"Tail gunner," answers the hawk-faced kid.

"But hadn't you heard," says the navigator. "This is Butt-End Charlie. Never knows where he's going, but can always tell you where he's been. Sits back there all alone, sprinkling Jerry fighters when they come smelling around our back side too intimately."

"Afraid I've got to be climbing in now," said the hawk-faced kid. "Glad to've met you. Luck," and he mounted the ladder.

"Matter of fact, about that sweater," the pilot shouted confidentially in my ear, "rather a good thing he did to get that. Happened last week. We'd been on daylight patrol over toward the Dutch coast and were coming back when a Jerry fighter dived on us and popped our starboard motor, and of course we knew we'd have to pancake on the sea. We made rather a good landing though if I do say it, but of course these planes float only a few minutes. We were so busy unfolding our dinghy and chucking it in the water we didn't notice the Jerry had followed us down. Nasty type, he was, all set to machine-gun us—maybe hoped to rip open the dinghy. Only just then there was a rat-tat-tat-tat-tat from the tail of our own plane. You see Butt-End Charlie had noticed the Jerry following us down. So instead of crawling on down into the main cockpit to be sure of getting in the dinghy, he'd stayed just a minute longer to pop the Jerry a last one. Brought him down, too. He plummeted into the water about a mile from us. As it was, Butt-End Charlie just managed to get clear of the plane before it sank, and we hauled him into the dinghy. The C.O.'s got a report on it at headquarters. Well, we must be going. See you later."

And he climbed the ladder. The trap door closed. The ground crew took the blocks away from the big wheels. We moved clear. At the end of the field we could see the first of the twelve Whitleys coming toward us down the center of the runway. Now its wheels are clear, now its whole silhouette is above the horizon, it is growing bigger and bigger, and suddenly it roars directly over us, the tops of the high trees at the edge of the airfield cringing backward from the force of the propeller blast.

"There goes number one," said the conducting officer.

"Which one is this?" and I jerk a thumb at the near-by Whitley plane. It is already beginning to taxi down the field to rise into the wind.

"Number five," he says. "Nice chaps, aren't they?"

Five has turned now, taxiing away from us, so that through the transparent machine-gun turret I can just make out the silhouetted helmet of Butt-End Charlie among the cold little nozzles and bands of ammunition. Whether he waved or grinned I'll never know, for just then the propeller blast blew a torrent of dried grass and dust in our eyes. Then they were gone, getting smaller as they bumped down the field. The sun is low, and the long black shadows seem fringed with a diluted blood red. As we are about to get into our car, here comes number five down the field in its takeoff, and away over the trees toward Germany in a suddenly vanishing roar. Now it is very quiet.

"Yes," I say, "I thought they were very nice chaps. What do we do now?"

"Wait," says the conducting officer. "Lot of that to do at a bomber station. Some of it isn't fun."

We go back to the big lounge room adjoining the mess hall where other pilots are sitting around in big overstuffed leather chairs, some talking, some browsing through magazines. We join a group near the big fireplace—where there is no fire, because sparks up the big chimney might be seen in the blackout. Outside in the gathering dusk the twelve big Whitleys must have gained their altitude and are probably now leaving the English coast behind, headed into the darkness over the North Sea and the continental beaches far ahead. Butt-End Charlie, peering out through the ammunition bands of his round transparent turret, is probably looking backward at the crimson trailings of the sunset over England, maybe the last he will ever see.

But in here it is warm and comfortable. The pilots come quickly to their feet and pull up chairs for us. But temporarily the presence of a journalist dampens conversation. They explain that they were out last night—usual thing, just up the Rhine and over the Ruhr. Noth-

[137]

ing much happened, so now there's little to do but take it easy while the ground crew overhauls the big motors —they probably won't go out again till the end of the week. They're a little shy. But they want to know what America thinks about all this, and after I answer them, I get my own questions going. For instance, what's it like up there flying over Germany?

"For the most part bloody dull," says a pilot. "Of course on the way out you're looking sharp for the reflections of rivers and the dark bands which bridges make across them. Then there's usually a bit of muck thrown up by their ground batteries—but that's about all."

"Is German anti-aircraft shooting pretty good?"

"As good as anybody's. But pretty soon you get to know the patches where they're every good—where they've had plenty of practice and can place the shots close enough to rock you around and make you want to get out of there quick."

"Can you feel them?"

"Ra-*ther!* A big one, landing close, knocks the plane about like a bloody basket of potatoes." Raising his two hands he rocks them from one side to the other in a great lurching swing.

"How high does it come?"

"Higher than we can fly. Forty thousand, maybe more. But unless there's a lot of it you can watch for the flashes."

[138]

"Of the exploding shells?"

"Oh no—the flashes of the guns on the ground. You see, with a heavy bomb and petrol load, we'll be coming over about twelve thousand. So pretty soon Jerry's listening devices pick us up, we watch the ground sharp and, sure enough, there's a flash. After you've seen a few, you can tell whether the shell will come straight at you, or is aimed at a plane in the other end of the sky. If it is coming at you, you glance at your watch dial second hand and note the time." The boy glances down at his wrist watch. "Flying at twelve thousand, you know you have about thirteen seconds to get out of the way, because it will take that long for the shell, leaving the gun muzzle with the flash, to climb up where you are, so you can roll over on one wing and dive sidewise. See, now the thirteen seconds are up!" and he pulls the cuff of his blue tunic back down over the wrist watch. "It's really plenty of time to get out of the way. Jerry has his predictor stuff which plots the course of our plane, so that if everything else went well, his shell would burst, thirteen seconds later, on the exact spot where our plane would have been if we'd kept our course. But no one has invented a predictor which can calculate which way we're going to dodge after we see his ground flash."

"What else happens on a raid?"

"Really nothing much," insists the pilot. "We've told you it's bloody dull. Freddie here is navigator, while I'm at the controls. After Freddie has got us to the target area, and if Jerry isn't throwing up too much muck, Freddie crawls down onto the bomb-sight. Then he usually has me make a couple of runs over the target itself—just for practice, and to be sure we've allowed for wind drift before we unload on it—same way a chap boxing will spar a bit before he releases a hay-maker. After we've started the stuff on its way down of course all of us are keen on spotting the explosion flash which comes maybe half a minute later. It always seems like the devil of a long wait but naturally we want to know if we hit the exact spot on the target we were aiming for. That's all there is to bombing."

"So then you come back?"

"That's right. Then we can all relax, open up the thermos of tea, which is sometimes still hot, and all of us have a good drink out of the thermos jug lid, and eat the sandwiches. All except poor old Butt-End Charlie —that's Larry here—back on the tail gunner's seat. He's so far back we can't pass him any tea. But we always tell him over the intercommunicating telephones how good it is, don't we, Larry? Then Larry always tells us how bloody cold he is, back there in the tail all alone."

"But isn't it heated?"

"In theory," says Larry, "but not much of it ever gets back into the bloody tail. I suppose you saw the chap who got the sweater? That's Blake, friend of mine. He's Butt-

End Charlie on plane five of tonight's flight—he'll be needing his Very Royal sweater, you can be sure of that."

"Yes, but Butt-End Charlie really has all the fun," insisted the pilot. "He gets to look back and watch all the fires we've started. They usually don't get going good until we've left the target. So Butt-End sits looking back at where we've come from, telling us about how we did— whether they're little yellow fires or lovely big red ones which he can see sometimes even after they drop over the horizon, reflected up on the clouds. If we run into any trouble ahead, Butt-End Charlie would be the last to know —he hasn't a care in the world."

"I wonder how tonight's flight is doing?"

The pilot glanced down at his watch. "Probably working up the Rhine round about B——, maybe even approaching that second bend and wondering just how much flack they'll run into at D——. Jerry keeps a nasty little patch of it there."

"You know those chaps at D—— are getting annoyingly good. Last week they placed a couple so close that they kicked us around like a clothes hamper—almost rolled me off the bomb-sight. Don't mind saying I was rather glad to get out of there."

The pilot rather thought that the Jerries on the jetty at Hamburg did tighter shooting than the batteries around D——. From here the conversation led into an argument as to exactly what was the effective range of the cannon Jerry was building into the new Messerschmitt. It waxed hot, but it was so long and so technical that I sat in silence, understanding so little that I presently ceased to listen. Where was number five by now? If it had dodged the nasty patch of German anti-aircraft fire around D——, it should be forging on in the darkness past the forest. Had it already sighted the glint of the triangular lake in the moonlight? Had it already come low to pick up the faint line of the four-lane autobahn which would guide it on into the target area? Did an occasional fat stone German farmhouse leak a little light through a badly covered kitchen window, or were they completely alone up in the brilliance of a three-quarters moon, with the earth inky black below?

"I was thinking," said the conducting officer, "since we'll be making a night of it, that a cup of tea might help us keep awake. We could pick one up in the mess—maybe even a cup of coffee for you, since you're an American. After that we can stroll on over to Ops."

"What are Ops?"

"Operations room. Where the chaps are in contact with tonight's flight—getting reports. It's eight now—they should be hearing from some of them presently."

"What goes on in Ops?"

"Some of it's very hush-hush. Can't let you see that, or tell you about it. All of it is involved in the business of getting reports from them, guiding them back, and getting them safe on the ground at this or some other field."

"Won't they all come back to this?"

"Not necessarily. If some other field is closer and they're short of petrol, they're sent on in to it instead. Or one field may have a ground fog, and it's a ticklish business getting them through soup. Or sometimes there are Jerries about. All sorts of reasons."

Over my coffee I fell to wondering. What were the hush-hush matters? Did they bring bombers in on radio beams such as transport planes use in times of peace? Every American has read that German pilots are sent over England on such beams. But if the British use them to guide their empty bombers homeward, wouldn't the same beams also guide German planes straight in to bomb British airdromes? And wouldn't the Germans send out imitations of these British beams which would lure British bombers, almost empty of gas, over water or mountains and forests to death? Who knew but that the air over northern Europe teemed tonight with a clicking buzz of wireless signals, some true and some decoys, sent out by both sides?

The conducting officer glances at his watch. "Nine o'clock," he says, gulping down the rest of his tea. We step out into the blackout and walk along an endless path. We don't need a torch because the moon is high.

The outlines of near-by hangars are clear, but the horizon is dim and blurry.

"H-mm. Ground mist," comments the conducting officer. "I'd rather not see that."

"Why not?"

"Murderous stuff. Probably kills more good boys than anti-aircraft fire."

"How?"

"Maybe you'll see tonight."

Nine o'clock and plane number five should be near the target area—may even now be skimming in on a practice run before releasing. The moon from 12,000 feet should look to them almost as it does to us—but how much can they see on the ground? Are they taking now their bearing on the cathedral spire? And are the long regular buildings of the airplane factory easy to make out despite the camouflage?

We open a door and part blackout curtains, walk up a dim-lit staircase and then out into a large room. It's bare and functional—perhaps a dozen men sitting at pine desks, most of them wearing earphone headpieces. At the central desk a young flight lieutenant greets us cheerfully.

"All well so far." He picks up several slips from a box. Numbers one, two and six have each reported. "On target. That's pretty good for 9:15 o'clock. Must have had a nice little tail wind on the last hundred miles. But let's knock on wood—I don't want another night like Wednesday last."

"What happened then?"

"A grisly business—but I suppose that's what you writing chaps want, isn't it? A flight had gone over to drop a few on the Stavanger Airport in Norway. On the way back they got mixed into a big electric storm—must have thrown their compasses out—blew them pretty well off course. They all got straightened out but one chap, and we couldn't get contact with him. He'd been blown clear out into the North Sea between Scotland and Holland. Except that the poor devil had no idea where he was—he thought he was on the other side of Scotland, and so was heading due east, expecting to sight Scotland any minute, although his petrol was almost gone.

"The grisly thing about it was that we could hear him, but he couldn't hear us. So we had to sit here listening to the poor chap—he was reporting every ten minutes—absolutely sure he was flying toward Scotland, telling us just what airdrome he hoped to come down on, assuring us he would have plenty of gas to make it, very confident, and we listening to him knowing that he was not in the Irish Sea but in the North Sea headed toward Germany, without enough petrol even to take him to Holland where he might get captured."

"What happened?"

"Finally we got through to him. Got him turned

around and headed back toward England, but by that time both he and we knew that he had so little petrol left he didn't have a chance. Of course we sent out an alarm, got out all the motor speed boats from all along the coast, had them combing the North Sea with searchlights. He sent us his last position just as his motors began to sputter, along with a message that the chaps in the plane all felt fine and not to kick up too much fuss about them—they'd pull through all right. That was the last we heard. Bloody fine chap he was, too."

"Were they able to land on the sea and get out into their dinghy?"

The young flight lieutenant shook his head. "The motor boats couldn't get a trace of them. North Sea's a pretty big place, you know. I'd rather tonight wasn't like Wednesday last."

He took a slip of paper from the hand of an orderly who had just come in.

"Another reporting on target—number five."

As I sat there, I kept thinking of the kid in the new blue pullover sweater under his flying suit, hanging high in the air over central Europe. Would he know when the crew forward in the cockpit pulled the bomb release levers? Of course he would, because as each bomb dropped away, the plane would bob upward, released from part of its load. But over the motor roar he couldn't hear them start to whistle as they gained momentum.

And about twenty seconds after each upward surge of the plane, there would be a quick white flash far below on the ground.

The flight lieutenant takes another slip from the orderly.

"Two more reporting on target—numbers three and four. That makes half a dozen in all and it's now nine-twenty. Ruddy good navigating, you know. I suppose they told you this is the longest flight we've made since the war began. Jerry's moving his factories further and further east, to get them away from us. But our chaps would be game to go out and smack a Heinkel factory, even if the Jerry begins moving them over into Russia. Only way to stop the filthy mess Jerry's making in London, you know. All right for civilians to talk about bombing Berlin. Chaps who really know realize a few stickfuls of bombs laid across their production lines are better. Smash their nests so they can't hatch new ones. Hello"—he reads a slip which has just arrived—"number eight is just reporting over target and it's just 9:30. Bloody good—really is, you know, considering the distance."

"How many more are there to hear from?"

"That's the lot for tonight. Seven out of twelve is better than I expected, considering the distance."

"What about the others?"

"Probably ran into headwinds and saw they couldn't make it. They carried an unusually heavy bomb load tonight and their petrol will only last nine hours. They took off at five, and their orders were that if they hadn't reached the target by 9:30, they were to turn back and unload on the secondary targets on the way home."

"Will more reports be coming in?"

"Not until about one o'clock. You see after they leave the target, they're under wartime silence until they have passed the Dutch coast and are well out over the North Sea. Come back then, and if this little ground fog thickens, we might have a bit of that sort of news you writing chaps are so keen on."

His smile was courteous, and yet it made me uncomfortable.

Back in the big lounge, we found most of the pilots had gone to bed, but three were still around the fireplace finishing an argument. This concerned a wind-current you sometimes encounter in a certain Alpine pass as you cross over to bomb the Fiat works near Milan. The red-headed kid argued that if you could get up to 14,000, the current would never bother you. The very slender one said it would bother you at any altitude, but only if there was a southwesterly wind.

Then they went to bed, and the conducting officer and I began browsing through a tattered pile of back numbers of *Sketch* and *Picture Post*. A thousand miles away out in the darkness the crew of number five had left their target behind them. Maybe Butt-End Charlie was looking off back at the fires they started. Only probably there were none. After all this wasn't a gasoline dump or a city—there would be little to burn in an aircraft factory, so after the winking flashes on the ground, there had probably been only blackness.

"I say, it's a long time till one o'clock," said the conducting officer. "Maybe you could do with a few winks here. We may be up the better part of the night if things don't go right." He drew his feet up on the upholstered davenport.

"Don't you think they will?"

"I don't know," he said. "There's this to be said for the airforce—if something nasty is going to happen you never know in advance so you don't worry. Also the nasty things are usually over quick, in a nice clean way."

He closed his eyes. I reached up and turned out the reading light over my shoulder.

Out there in the darkness over central Germany the four boys in the cockpit would be unscrewing their thermos bottle full of hot tea, milk and sugar, and filling the top and passing it around. Or maybe unwrapping the thick sandwiches. And probably asking Butt-End Charlie, over their intercommunicating phones, if it was really as cold back there in the tail as he insisted it was. Were they fumbling their way back along the autobahn and thence down the Rhine? Probably not. Since they had found and left their target, they might as well head straight for England on a compass-bearing. What would they talk about during those three monotonous hours, while Hitler's blacked-out Reich slowly drifted two or three miles below them under the transparent screen of the bomb-sight? Lightened of both their bombs and half their gasoline, might they not see the low moonlight glinting on the flat Dutch beaches before one o'clock? Nine hours is a long time to spend hanging crouched in the aluminum entrails of a bomber, swinging high over an enemy land, with the big motors roaring on, hour after hour!

And now then someone is shaking my shoulder. I've slept three hours and it's time to go back to the operations room. It is very dark outside because the moon is about to set, and a light ground mist is writhing and sworling like smoke across its yellow face.

The flight lieutenant at the desk gave us a nod.

"What does it look like?" asked the conducting officer.

"A bit on the filthy side," said the flight lieutenant. "I suppose you noticed the mist."

"Yes."

"Just enough to put a fuzz over everything for the chaps coming in. In addition the coast watchers report a couple of Jerries mucking about in Yorkshire—can't tell when they may alter course and move up this way."

"But what could they do up here? There are no cities near."

"They could try to follow our chaps in, watch for the landing flare path to come on, and lay a stickful across our hangars."

"You mean bomb us?" I asked.

"I believe it's customary," said the flight lieutenant dryly.

"What news of the chaps out tonight?"

"Three of them back already. Found they couldn't make the primary target so they unloaded on the secondaries and came home. We brought them in at X—— (he named an airfield fifty miles away) because this filthy ground mist hadn't reached there yet, although it was on its way. A couple more also had to unload on secondaries and come back early. They haven't crossed the English coast yet but we're bringing them down here because the station at X—— now reports ground mist even thicker than ours."

"How about the other seven?"

"What word we have is all right. Most of them have passed the Dutch coast on their way in, but it will be a ruddy close shave on petrol—they've been fighting headwinds for the past two hours over Germany. It will be touch-and-go getting them safe on the ground before their motors begin to sputter. That's the news so far. You chaps might have a look at the night." Here he nodded

[151]

at a heavily curtained maze at one end of the room. Threading our way through this, we came to a door, which opened on a balcony.

Before our eyes became used to the darkness we saw only the moon drifting through sworling low mist. Then I noticed we were not alone on the balcony. A uniformed and steel-helmeted lookout was standing almost at our elbow. Then gradually we could make out, through the haze, the furry outlines of two near-by hangars, and the great expanse of the landing field in front. But the dark line of forest which marked its other end was wrapped in this death shroud of mist. Looking straight up, the stars came through to us dimly.

"They'll be coming in presently," said the conducting officer.

"Excuse me, sir, just a minute," said the lookout. He was listening intently.

Sure enough there it was, off to the left, very faint, the nasal whine of a bomber. The lookout stepped behind us through the door into the curtain maze.

"A bit early, you know," said the conducting officer, "and it's rather funny that they're coming in from so far north."

Suddenly the bomber noise was drowned by the grind of an automobile starter just under our balcony, and then the hum of an automobile motor. Beneath us was the dim outline of a large covered truck.

"Starting up the crash wagon," explained the conducting officer. "That's part of getting ready."

"What's a crash wagon?"

"Combination ambulance and light fire-wagon. They have hoses and chemicals to smother fires, asbestos suits and first aid bandages. Every now and then on a thick night like this a pilot will smash his landing gear, nose over and catch fire. The crash wagon goes rushing over to pull the chaps out if they can. Watch the field now, because they'll be turning on the landing lights any minute."

The door behind us opened very suddenly and the sentinel jostled us aside. "Which one of the planes is that?" asked the conducting officer.

"None of them, sir," and then he leaned over the rail to shout at the crash wagon below. "Hey, you chaps—cut your motor."

"Wot's up?" came the voice from below.

"Bloody Jerry plane up there." The motor died and now we could hear the whine of the Heinkel, moving toward us.

"I wonder if he can see these hangars."

"Couldn't say. We'll know in a minute if things start whistling down. Rather doubt it, though—he's pretty high. Bloody good thing we didn't switch on our flare path or he certainly would have laid a stick of bombs across the field. Don't want any of that, you know. Our chaps will have enough to get down at all tonight without worrying about nosing over into craters."

The noise was now almost overhead. That meant that the plane had already passed over us. The bombs, if any were to fall, had already been released. In a few seconds we would hear whistles, if there were to be any. All of us knew this, and stood listening. But there was only a great stillness from the fog-shrouded field, under that angry hum from the high sky. Looking up we could see only the sickly stars. Slowly the hum passed over and dwindled. The Heinkel had not sighted our hangar. Its high snarl faded into the southern end of the sky. Meanwhile what was going on inside? We fumbled through the blackout curtains.

"Close, wasn't it?" said the flight lieutenant, smiling grimly. "Better step back out there, because one of our chaps is over the coast on his way in. They're sending them all to us for the present, because the field at X—— is now closed down tight. Fog rolling in about a thousand feet thick, visibility zero. Of course it may shift."

"Are you going to bring him in now?"

"Going to tell him to circle the field a few times at about five thousand, to give that Jerry time to get out of the way so he can't see our flare path when we switch it on. Provided, of course, our chap has the petrol to circle."

"Where are the rest?"

"Two more about fifteen minutes behind him."

"Will they bring them on in here?"

"Depends on how much thicker it gets here. May send them on up the coast to Y——. It was blotted out an hour ago but on last reports it seemed to be thinning. Headquarters is operating on a minute-to-minute basis, depending on information it receives from each station."

From above came a long-drawn groan which sent us back through the curtains and out onto the balcony. Again it was pitch black until our eyes became used to the darkness, while from above came the groans in huge circles as the bomber spiraled. They were the long, low, even moans of some great animal in a death agony. Tben they almost died away as the sound receded. The curtains behind us fluttered as the young flight lieutenant stepped out on the balcony.

"Bringing him on in now," he said. The hum of motors was returning, was louder, was almost a roar. And suddenly we saw the plane against the white of the fog— a swift-gliding black shape, and at that instant the flare path came on. It was very frightening. You could not see the individual electric bulbs which dotted the field; each one, through the fog, seemed a faintly luminous ball of cotton, but nevertheless we seemed suddenly and rather horribly exposed. For here, in this blacked-out island of England, long after midnight, these particular acres out of the millions suddenly leaped into view,

picked out by these fluffy lights which could plainly be
seen by any wandering German miles away.

"Which is it, sir?" asked the lookout.

"Number six—Simmonds," answered the flight lieutenant.

"Won't be easy for him—he's a bit new at this. Who-o-
o-oap!—loook o-o-out!"

The big plane, its landing gear down, seemed to have
cleared the roof of a hangar by inches—now it was settling down into the maze of landing lights. Just below
us we heard the motor of the crash wagon start. The
plane was teetering unsteadily, settling, its big wheels feeling uncertainly for the ground, lower into the little balls
of luminous cotton, then bounce as the wheels first
touched ground. Now the long tapering tail was settling— "He made it!" said the lookout exultantly.

The flight lieutenant turned back through the curtains.

"Flare path out," we heard him call. Instantly the luminous balls of cotton vanished and there was only the roar
of the bomber's motors in the darkness. These presently
became huge, self-satisfied snorts as the plane taxied un-
evenly back down the field to its hangar. The crew of
the crash wagon cut their little motor into silence.

But where was five? Maybe one of the two coming in
now, the light of the setting moon on its undercarriage.
Looking down on the airdrome, what would the tail
gunner see? Only a fluffy blanket of white—an occasional

high wisp gleaming brighter in the moonlight—with maybe the dark roof of a hangar protruding through this thin death shroud of ground mist which lay so lightly on our field, with the flare path, when it came on, gleaming dully beneath it like an orange candlewick pattern on a cotton-batting quilt. Down into this fluffy shroud they would have to sink, hoping and trusting presently to feel the gentle bump of firm earth against the undercarriage wheels.

And suddenly I hear it—a low buzz off to the east.

"There they are," says the lookout. Only is it off to the east? For half a minute it seems to be coming from the south—but then again there it is, distinctly in the east again. Probably an echo in the fog. The flight lieutenant who has again come out on the balcony listens intently.

"That's three and four," he says. "We'll let four circle while we bring three in first." But an orderly suddenly bursts through the curtains onto the balcony.

"That Jerry that went off south—Station P reports they heard him turn a bit ago, headed back this way, sir."

"All right, tell them no flare path. Tell the sergeant to make contact again with three and five and ask them both to circle, find out how much petrol they have left, tell them there's a Jerry buggering about, and we may have to send them down to Z——. Query Z—— and ask for another report on field conditions."

He listened another minute and went back inside. The

chill silvery mist above us seemed to writhe with great swirling groans as the bombers circled—the air muttered and moaned in travail.

"One's probably been told to circle at five thousand, the other at six, to avoid collision," said the conducting officer.

"Where's the Jerry?"

"Could be any place mixed in among them—maybe above them, since he probably doesn't suspect he's over an airdrome."

"Can't he see the two planes circling?"

"Sky's a pretty big place at night, particularly when everybody's buzzing around at better than a hundred miles an hour. A chance though, that he's glimpsed one of them from above, silhouetted against this bloody white ground mist. If he has, he's probably following it around, and will follow it down when it comes in to land, and drop a stick of bombs along its landing line. We won't have long to wait."

The flight lieutenant comes back through the curtains to peer at the grinding, moaning night sky.

"The field at Z—— is shut down tight—better than a thousand feet of ground mist against less than a hundred for us. Our only chance is to get them down here. Number three's all right—they report they have petrol for half an hour. The Jerry should be gone by then."

"What about four?"

"Doesn't answer. Something gone wrong with their wireless. Think they hear us all right because they're still circling, but the point is, do they have petrol to circle for another hour, or another minute?" His voice was even but very strained. "Be nice if we knew."

But something was happening up in the black sky. We all listened. The sworling grind was still there, but at only about half its intensity.

"One of 'em's gone," said the squadron leader intensely. "Probably number four—knows his petrol's about done and it's now or not at all—probably gone out to circle down and make a run in for the field with his last gallon."

"Going to give him a flare path?"

"How can I? That Jerry's still mucking about—hear him?—and we've another plane waiting to come in and more just back."

"Isn't number four Allenby, sir?" asked the sentinel.

"That's right."

"If anybody can make it without lights, Allenby can."

"Crash wagon on the ready!" shouted the flight lieutenant over the balcony, and then slipped inside the curtains.

"Allenby's one of our best," continued the sentinel. "Sets a Whitley down gentle as a baby, Allenby does. Knows this field like the palm of 'is 'and. If the roof of just one 'angar is stickin' up through this bloody muck

[159]

of a mist, that's all the bearings Allenby'll need to ease 'er down on the field. I 'ope."

From the south comes a far-away buzz, rapidly increasing to a roar. A little sword of light stabs the darkness for about a second, then winks out. Again it winks on and off as the plane hurtles by.

"Doin' a big figure eight, 'e is—feelin' for the ground with 'is landing spotlight. 'E'll be back in a minute, make another turn, and then, if I know Allenby, 'e'll try to set 'er down." Again the big bomber hurtles by. It's only a black shape in the mist, with the spotlight coming out from the underside of its nose, stabbing forward and a little downward at the field, winking off and on. The roar diminishes but never ceases as the big bomber makes its final turn.

"All right! Now 'e'll do it! It's now or never!"

Now we see the plane, and I grip the iron railing of the balcony as tightly as I ever gripped the railing of a box at a mystery play, for there it is, a black shape floating directly across our line of vision, smoothly, evenly—the landing spotlight in its nose gleams for a second, forward and downward, prodding for the ground like a blind man's stick—blackness and then another prod. The glide of the big plane is so steady that we cannot tell at what instant the wheels have touched the ground.

" 'E done it, 'e did!" cried the sentinel. " 'E can bring one of them big Whitleys in, steady as a muckin' church, and smooth 'er down over the grass soft and easy as you or me runnin' our 'and up past our sweet'eart's knee!— beggin' your pardon, sir."

The conducting officer turned to me. "Think we'd better be getting over to Intelligence. When the chaps come in from a flight they're always questioned as to what happened during the night. Give you a chance to see how we decide what goes into next morning's Air Ministry communiqué." I follow him through the curtains and we pause by the desk of the flight lieutenant, rather wishing we could wait here until number five was safe.

The dozen men with headphones and eyeshades are all busy, most of them talking intently into mouthpieces. It looks as efficient as the control tower of a great switching yard, but connected directly or indirectly with these earphones and mouthpieces are wires or radio beams which link with every other airforce station in Britain— with the Air Ministry at Whitehall—with planes buzzing in over the North Sea or in the dark heart of Germany. Here are a few cells in that vast electrical brain which is the General Staff of Britain's Army of the Midnight Air. There are broken scraps of conversation:

"Sorry—sorry—can't handle them here—suggest you send them south." "A line to Whitehall please—if you can't connect me direct tell them we've just picked up Flight Z at a bearing of O-eight-nine—I repeat—O-eight-nine." "Please notify ground forces at J—— that a hostile plane passed over five minutes ago headed southeast, altitude 12,000."

Here in this babble of technical jargon were men working under great strain—and yet always with that unfailing British courtesy which somehow reveals the steady nerves of the breed, and which somehow feels more dependable in a real crisis than the more glittering types of crisp and brittle efficiency. Through the growling darkness (a plane is still groaning overhead) we walk over to Intelligence headquarters.

The wheel has turned full circle. We are back in the classroom but now it is almost empty. The plump wing commander, jovial no longer, is at his desk. On either side are two other officers, taking notes. In front of them stand five boys, still in their flying suits and holding their helmets in their hands. We sit down in the back of the room, by the side of another intelligence officer.

"You arrived over target when?"

"At 9:28, sir. We circled for about fifteen minutes. The whole valley was full of mist, completely covering the target area. The hills on either side were sticking up like islands. After making sure of this, we came on back to unload on the secondary target."

"When did you first sight the fog?"

"Just as we were passing over the forest. It was creeping up through the trees like skimmed milk."

"Did you see the two lakes?"

"Yes, sir. Passed directly over the triangular one at about 10,000 feet. We could see it plainly, no fog there."

"Directly over? You should have passed to the right of it. Sure you mightn't have picked up the wrong autobahn?"

"Don't think so, sir. Because when we got in, we took five runs over the area and took two sights, both of which showed we were directly on target."

"I think you said the fire at the secondary target broke out immediately."

"That's right, sir. Rather think it must have been a goods train of oil or petrol cars on a siding. There was no doubt we were over the yards, because we could see the glint of the steel rails very plainly in the moonlight."

"Did the firing start when you came over target?"

"No, sir. We made three runs and I think the ground crews must have presumed we were one of theirs. There were no ground flashes until about fifteen seconds after we saw our own explosions. But the firing from there was much heavier than last week. I'd say that target is now twice as well defended as it was, judging by the flack they chucked up at us."

"That's all for tonight. Thank you. Call in the next."

The five boys filed out and five more came in. The young faces, under the hair tousled by the helmets, looked tired and serious. Yet it was hard to believe that

I was watching the striking forces of one great world Empire who were reporting on a raid into the dark heart of another.

Standing there in their flying suits with their helmets in their hands, they looked so much more like football players called on the carpet by their coach, to report on just what happened during the crucial quarter of a big football game.

The faces are vaguely familiar, but this isn't the crew of number five. And by the way, where is five? But before I can ask the conducting officer, the report begins.

Yes, the trip up the Rhine was without incident, only a little anti-aircraft fire passing over D——. They saw the triangular lake on the left clearly, had no trouble picking up the autobahn at the edge of the forest, and this brought them into the target area at 9:32. Taking a bearing on the cathedral spire, they'd located the target with no trouble—

"What," interrupts the wing commander at his desk, "were weather conditions over the target area?"

"Clear, sir. A few light cumulus wisps at about 8,000. We made our first run over the target at about 10,000. As we turned back for our second run, we saw ground flashes, and when we came in for our third to unload the flack was popping. But it was exploding at least 2,000 feet above us—didn't bother us much. The factory was very clear in the moonlight—nice rectangular buildings in orderly rows—might have been a barracks, it was so neat. We laid a stick diagonally across it. Think one bomb struck the big central building."

"No ground mist whatever?"

"No, sir, quite clear. We were off target by 9:40 and got in ten minutes ago. Only other thing we saw was rather a good fire going just down the coast from Antwerp. Must have been started by some of the other chaps."

"But visibility over target was good?"

"Excellent, sir. Noticed a heavy low cloud bank about a hundred miles off to the southeast, but the target area itself was clear."

Yet the next crew to report was equally sure that the target valley had been level full of mist, while the one which followed it, the last to report, insisted that visibility had been excellent.

As they filed out, we rose. The intelligence officer turns to me. "Sorry that spoils your story. Three of the planes reported they bombed the aircraft factory at T——, but the other three insisted the target area was covered with fog. So officially we didn't bomb T—— tonight."

"But the first three were so sure!"

"Unofficially, I'm convinced they did bomb T——. But it's three against three. That's not enough. So tomorrow morning the Air Ministry communiqué will only say that twelve planes of the bomber command successfully raided objectives in the Ruhr, starting fires in the goods yards at H——, and that all our aircraft returned to base."

"But it can't be three against three. Because seven planes in all reported off target. What about number five? Did they find fog? Have they reported yet?"

"No," said the intelligence officer.

"Haven't they returned yet?"

"Oh yes," said the intelligence officer. "They were killed about twenty minutes ago trying to land at Z——. Didn't have the petrol to make it on up here."

"You mean number five—the plane whose little tail gunner got the sweater this afternoon?"

"Blake. Nice chap, wasn't he? Rather keen on my kid sister. Spends most of his leaves visiting her at our place in Surrey. Spent, I mean. But of course we've no way of knowing what they saw over target, so with number five out, that leaves it three against three. Officially we won't claim to have bombed T—— tonight."

14 . MARGARET : V

THERE is a little crisis at the Rest Center. Mrs. Swope, the foster mother for the adoption society, who lives in Maida Vale, has telephoned to ask if the children will both stay at the Rest Center over Christmas, which is tomorrow. She wonders because she had expected them back, and had prepared a little Christmas party for them.

What shall she do with their presents—send them or keep them?

Hedy explains to me that the tests won't be held until after Christmas. The children must have plenty of time to relax before any test would be fair. And yet maybe it would be wise if the children went back to this foster mother, at least for the party. Because maybe one or both might fail the tests, and if eventually they must go back, they shouldn't be allowed to forget Mrs. Swope—the return would be too hard on them. So would I take them to the party tomorrow? Because, since they're used to me, it would be much easier on them. I agree, and so Hedy explains to John and Margaret that just for tomorrow, I will take them back to Mrs. Swope, who has a beautiful Christmas party prepared for them.

"I don't want to go," says John, beginning to look frightened.

"But such a beautiful party! Mummy Swope likes John and Margaret so much."

"No!" says Margaret, beginning to cry.

"You wouldn't want John and me to leave you here?" I contribute, "all alone?"

"Yes," says Margaret, "with Hedy."

"I want to stay too," says John, beginning to whimper.

"Such a lovely party!" insists Hedy. "And Mummy Swope loves you both so much, and has worked so hard, and has such nice presents!"

"I want to stay here!" wails Margaret.

"But, Margaret," says Hedy, "Mr. White will take you in a taxi, a proper motor car, and bring you back—we promise."

"No!" wails Margaret.

At eleven I arrive with my taxi at 13 Wedderburn Road. Immediately the door opens. Over the children's heads Hedy smiles at me and then shakes her own helplessly. Margaret is bundled up in her little red coat, leggings and her red pixie hood. John wears his schoolboy's cap and blue overcoat.

"Such sad faces we have today!" mourns Hedy. The

children hang on Hedy's fingers, as unwilling feet fumble down the stone steps.

Margaret turns her face upward. "Is it the truf he'll bring me back?"

"Yes, dear, it's the truth."

"Will I see?"

"Oh yes, you'll see."

Slowly, sadly, skeptically, she gets into the taxi and then whimperingly crawls up on my lap, puts a tense arm around my neck. There is no love in that gesture. It is stiff with fear.

John sits morose, with no interest in bomb craters.

The Swopes turned out to be nice, simple people who lived in a spick and span little house—not a scratch on the varnish of the new parlor suite.

The whole thing was so sweetly planned, down to the last perfect fold of the paper napkins with colored Mother Goose figures—it cried out for responsive appreciation. Maybe too loudly.

John wouldn't look at Mrs. Swope. Margaret looked. Then, loudly and clearly, "When do we go back?"

"After lunch, dear," I said, "and now we'll take your leggings and pixie off—"

"I don't *want* to!"

"But, Margaret, we're in the house now."

"When do we go back?" asks John.

"In an hour."

"Why don't we go back now?"

"Why, Margaret, you haven't seen the be-e-a-utiful presents," and I reach for the top button.

"No!" shouts Margaret, "I don't want them off!"

"The pretty, pretty presents—" I continue. John at least has let Mrs. Swope take off his overcoat. Margaret won't part even with her overshoes.

In the living room Mrs. Swope introduces her daughter, a very beautiful girl of twelve, and her son of eighteen. The girl is the first child Mrs. Swope ever cared for. She and her husband liked her so much they adopted her themselves. Margaret crawls firmly up in my lap and starts to cry when I try to put her down.

"What's this—for Margaret!" I exclaim. "Don't you want to unwrap it?"

"You," she says sullenly.

The Swopes are clustered round, anxiously. "What do you suppose it is? What can it be? Why, a dolly! A dolly with yellow hair, just like Margaret's!"

"When will we go back?" asks Margaret. I would like to turn her lovingly upside down and break the dolly over her stubborn little bottom! The bewildered Swopes look at me sadly.

Now dinner. A snowy white tablecloth and the places all set. In the center a holly wreath, from the ceiling dangle some of those gay colored noise-makers the British call crackers, designed to delight children. Normal

children that is, not these. Margaret climbs up on my lap
and refuses to get down, so I must feed her. The menu
starts with orange juice, which must have cost a pretty
penny. I haven't seen a dozen oranges in the island since I
came. There is jelly omelet with buttered toast, and half
of a plump golden peach with cake.

"Will we go back soon?" asks Margaret.

"When you've eaten your cake."

"I don't like the cake!"

She draws a deep breath and lets out a long, heart-
broken howl, and another, until her little face is purple.

"What is it?" I ask, stern but anxious.

"You—won't—leave me?" Each word comes out between hiccoughs and piercing wails.

"Oh no. I said I'd take you back."

"To—Hedy?"

"Back to Hedy."

"Is—that—the—truf? Will—I—see?"

"You'll see."

"You—won't—leave—me—with—her?" She points her
little forefinger, with a baleful look in her streaming
black eyes, at the startled Mrs. Swope.

In the taxi Margaret no longer needs to sit in my lap.
She stands with John by the window, shouting over the
wonderful game of which can first see a bomb crater as
we pass.

[171]

"It is almost cruel to them that we should know so well here how to make them happy," comments Hedy, "because then it is so hard for them when they must leave."

15. MINE-SWEEPER

THE mine-sweeping trawler which will presently take me out into the English Channel is waiting below at the quai, but meanwhile I stand here and look out toward the blue water from this most dramatic little bit of coastline in the world—the erstwhile sleepy town of Dover, from which fat channel steamers, crammed with tourists, once left for Paris. But Dover today is the jumping-off-place of the democratic world.

Standing here on its waterfront, with the medieval tile-roofed town and the chalk cliffs at your back, you look across less than twenty miles of glistening blue water toward the low, irregular purple coastline which was once France, but which the people of Dover now jocularly call *Deutsch Europa*.

Stare long enough at this irregular purple line and you will see a quick, whitish-yellow flash. This means that a shell from one of the Nazi long-range guns has started on its journey toward England. It also means that you have one minute and twenty seconds to take cover before the

[173]

shell arrives, or to brace your nerves, stand your ground and see what damage it does. In that interval the Nazi shell, rising steeply, soars fourteen miles above the blue channel, loses impetus and begins falling until, by the time it reaches Dover, it is dropping in almost a perpendicular line, like a fat raindrop.

The good people of Dover, about half of whom still live in their town, complain bitterly in their pubs over their pale ale that the shells strike without a preliminary whistle or scream—so you don't know when to duck unless you stand all day with your eyes glued to the coast of *Deutsch Europa,* which no one in busy Dover has time to do.

Yet these shells do surprisingly little damage. Each must have enormously thick walls to stand the crushing explosive charge which starts it on its journey—fourteen miles up—twenty miles across. So there is room only for a small charge of cordite within the shell. When it lands, it can do little more than tear out a single wall from one room.

The spectacular damage in Dover—there isn't much— has all been done by bombers. The long range guns are only a minor nuisance. It is true, of course, that the shells for the most part are aimed at vessels within and outside Dover harbor. But if the Nazis boast their guns now command the channel, the British can retort that no one need heed such commands because, so far, with convoys passing on schedule through the straits and trawlers regularly sweeping for mines, the long range guns have failed to scratch a single British ship.

The tremendous cost of maintaining them—each gun must be sent back to its Rhineland factory to be re-bored after about eighty shots—is out of all proportion to their nuisance value.

Dive bombers—one of them swooped to machine-gun all Dover's fat balloons in ten minutes—are another matter, but there is always the R.A.F. and, standing on this waterfront, you see it carving its initials in the sky over the channel, a bold handwriting in big loops of frozen steam against the blue. Almost every day it is possible to stand on this stone pier and watch the best men in England die beautifully and gracefully in the sky above.

Here, from the direction of *Deutsch Europa* two squadrons of German planes, too high to tell what they are—probably Messerschmitt 110s, each carrying a single bomb—are moving in one oblong, coffin-like formation, flying high, at least 20,000. But then from above first one, then two more, now at least half a dozen Spitfires drop on them. And as the six curving streaks of frozen steam descend on the flying coffin formation, its hard outlines waver and then dissolve. Now it has no more shape than a swarm of bees as the Messerschmitts scatter in disorderly route.

One dog-fight detaches itself from the squirming mass

just above. You can't see the planes, except now and then a glint as the sun catches their wings. You see only two threads of frozen steam, slowly braiding round and round each other. But after ten minutes one thread starts straight downward toward the channel waters while the victorious plane moves off. This means a dead pilot, whether British or German I cannot know. But the record of his last desperate minute hangs above me in the sky, slowly dissolving, but still plain to read half an hour after he has struck the water.

Here in the waters and skies of Dover you read the answer to the question of why the Nazis have not invaded England. The big guns and the bombers have not yet given them control of that 20-mile strip of water which is the key to the island.

But now the trawler is waiting, and I must go aboard.

"A very fine little doggie!" says the old chief of staff, taking the little toy dachshund into his arms. She turns her little black eyes up to his blue ones, sticks out a thin little pink tongue in a vain attempt to lick his shaggy gray eyebrows above her, and then turns her wet shiny little nose onto his coat sleeve, sniffing the many rings of gold braid which indicate his exalted rank.

"Her name is Bombproof Bella," says the captain. "She's the mascot of the trawler. Made every trip with the *Stella Orion* since I was given command. Been dive-bombed, machine-gunned, blown about by mines. Simply loves 'em. Gives tongue like a foxhound when we explode one. Never makes a mistake. Can tell a mine a thousand yards away."

But Bombproof Bella, bored with this recital of her charms, was gazing at the chalk cliffs of Dover which rise back of the town. Then she inspects the smoke coming from the funnel of the trawler *Stella Orion* which is tied up to the quai on which we stand.

"If you don't mind, sir," said the captain, "I think I'd better take Bella down the ladder. I stuff her inside my coat and she has learned a way of hanging on, buttoned in there with her paws around my neck."

Grasping the ropes of the ladder which were tied to a steel beam, the captain lowers himself over the side of the quai with Bombproof Bella peeping out at us with the reproachfully forgiving eyes of a dachshund. Then we follow him down the ladder to the greasy deck of the stout little *Stella Orion,* once a fishing boat which supplied the British public with those fish and chips which are the English equivalent of hot dogs and hamburgers, and now commissioned a mine-sweeping trawler in the service of the Royal Navy.

We walk along the deck stepping over piles of coiled rope and reels of cable and finally climb to the bridge which in peacetime was the roof of the wheelhouse. Only now it has been provided with an armored steel railing.

Peering down over the port side I see a little steel-covered balcony out of which peeps an anti-aircraft machine-gun. There's another one just like it on the starboard side. Up ahead in the bow is another platform about as high as our bridge, and on it is a four-inch gun whose crew is lolling beside it, with their steel helmets cocked comfortably on the backs of their heads, smoking cigarettes and pitching the butts overside. Another gun platform and crew are back in the stern.

I look at the thick steel railing which encircles the bridge.

"And if we run onto a mine I suppose we duck somewhere behind this?"

"Never any time to duck," explains the first officer. "You'll be lighting a cigarette one second and in the next you'll find yourself flop in the cold sea, with no idea of how you got there. Matter of fact, chaps who've watched other chaps be blown up say they describe the most beautiful slow graceful arc before they hit the water. Only chaps who've been blown up themselves never remember anything until they hit the water. Rather a pity, because the view from the top of that arc must be rather good."

"Have you ever been blown up?"

"Only once. But chaps who've been blown up lots of times never remember any more than I did."

"I suppose you only duck down behind the railing when you're dive-bombed."

[178]

"Complete waste of time. Because you never know where a bomb is going to strike a ship and wouldn't know where to crouch. Might as well stand upright and watch the fun. But it's wonderful when you're being machine-gunned from the air. Then you know just from what direction the stuff is coming at you, and can do some efficient crouching."

The trawler is under way and we are now rounding a jetty. Dover harbor under its tall white cliff dwindles behind us. Ahead is the open channel water. In our wake comes a sturdy file of three other trawlers of which we are the flotilla leader.

Above the sharp and straight horizon line of the sea is an irregularly wavy dark line lying close down on the waters. The red-headed young first officer points to it. "There is *Deutsch Europa*," he says. The waters into which we now move are a no-man's-land in the war at sea. Above us the air is equally any-man's sky, for the blue is combed into great swirls of white by air battles which are constantly in progress.

The waters beneath this battleground are equally any-man's ocean. The German mine layers come out to sow the seeds of death in the shipping lane. Out among these we move now, hoping to harvest them from the sea lane to make it safe for the next regular convoy of precious merchant ships which must pass through this channel to London.

Entering these waters I get a feeling I have not had since one night a year ago in Finland, when we crept down a hillside out of a forest into an open valley between the lines where the snow was laced with ski tracks of Russian patrols. Back of me are law, order, courts, policemen, soldiers, everything which represents safety and the shelter of a government which has protected you all your life. Just ahead is another government which also has its laws, policemen and soldiers, but all of them bent on killing you if they see you.

For the present they don't see us. Or maybe they don't care. Perhaps they are only waiting. For whatever reason the ominous blue line of *Deutsch Europa* lies silent on the horizon.

The first officer follows my eyes and grins. "Might let us know if you notice any flashes coming from over there. A Hun battery fired more than a hundred shells at us last Wednesday. Maybe mistook us for a convoy, because they seldom bother with trawlers."

"How many ships did they hit?"

"They've never hit a ship yet, although one shell landed exactly in our wake not 20 yards astern. That's why we watch for flashes."

"What do you do when you see one?"

"Glance at your watch."

"Why does it matter what time it is?"

"It doesn't. You only glance at the minute hand so

you'll know when it's time to duck behind the railing."

"I don't think I follow."

"Very simple. From our present position the Hun's long range battery is 17 miles away. That gives you exactly one minute and fourteen seconds after you see the flash. Time to fumble out a cigarette and waste two matches lighting it before sauntering over to the shelter."

So at last we are trawling, a sport which combines the best features of flying a kite and harvesting a thousand acres of Kansas wheat. Our tackle is about 200 yards of steel cable unreeled over one side of the boat. Bobbing on the end of this is what seems to be a hollow floating tin fish slightly longer than a man. Suspended under this floating tin fish is something called a door for the logical reason that it is shaped like one, except that it is made of steel-thin steel plate.

And this so-called door is an under-water kite, attached to the ship by a cable as the kite is attached to the small boy who flies it by a string. Except this kite, being of steel, flies under water, being kept from sinking deeper than about 12 feet by the floating tin fish which bobs above.

On a day when there is little wind a small boy with a kite will provide a breeze by running. So our ship provides the water breeze for its kite by moving through the water. If the small boy runs rapidly, his kite moves in the air at an angle of 45 degrees or more to the ground. Likewise if we increase our speed our trawling apparatus (the door and float above it) will move out from the side of the ship until the cable, like the kite string, is stretched tautly at about a 45-degree angle with the wake of the ship.

Of course if the small boy runs too fast, or tries to fly his kite from the rear observation platform of a whizzing streamliner, the kite will jump wildly about in the wake of the speeding train and probably snap the string. And so with trawling. If the ship went too fast the steel door would leap wildly out of water and probably snap its cable. We must maintain an even speed.

But note the construction of this cable, for trawling is not a sport invented to keep the British Navy amused and out of mischief playing with submarine kites. It's a tough, thin little kite string woven of special steel which makes it act like an under-water saw—a cutting blade 200 yards long, moving edgewise through the water, and kept submerged at exactly 12 feet below the surface by the weight of the door to which it is attached which keeps it from rising, and by the float above the door which keeps it from sinking any deeper.

It is a submarine saw, cutting a swathe 200 yards wide—moving under the mines which the Nazi mine layers have carefully planted—cutting quickly through the cables which anchor the mines to the bottom, as you would snip off the thin stem of a toadstool, thus letting the mines come bobbing up to the surface where they can be destroyed.

I watch our little flotilla at work. We are the leading ship, our float is bobbing along parallel with us and only a little behind us, 200 yards out on the port side of the ship. Back of this bobbing float comes the second ship—its course is just inside the wake of our float, so the ship itself is traveling in water which we have swept clean, but the trawl from this second ship is extended another 200 yards out into dangerous water. The third ship travels just within the edge of the 200-yard ribbon of water swept by the second, the fourth ship comes along behind the third in the same position, so altogether the four ships sweep a wide band. Looking back at the four I realize that trawling an area of ocean is exactly like harvesting an ocean of wheat on the western Kansas prairies—where sometimes half a dozen wheat harvesting combine units travel around a single huge field, the tractor wheels of each combine crunching the edge of the stubble strip left by the one in front of it.

Only at precisely this point in my calculations, the bridge and ship suddenly shiver, as though a giant had unexpectedly chucked a blacksmith's anvil against the *Stella Orion*. Perhaps there was also some noise a few seconds later. I will never know, because Bombproof Bella, who has been lying curled up in the scuppers, promptly goes mad with delight, and opening her long brown little muzzle to disclose her rosebud-pink tonsils, screams with joy. Then I see, about halfway between the side of our ship and the bobbing tin fish, a tall column of water rise into the air. It's about the size and shape of the ghost of a thin and dignified Sunder School Superintendent. As I watch, the ghost of the Sunday School Superintendent subsides languidly back into the sea with a churning splatter.

"Damn," says the first officer, and shouts an order down the speaking tube which stops our engines.

"Was that a mine?" I ask. Then I notice that our tin fish is no longer leaping through the waves abreast of us, but is rolling listlessly and dropping rapidly astern. Its cable must be broken.

"Bloody bore!" he says, scowling. "That was an explosive cutter."

"What's an explosive cutter?"

"Filthy little thing contrived by Jerry for the special purpose of irking His Majesty's mine-sweepers."

"But just what is it?"

"We aren't allowed to say exactly. Naval secrets and all that, rather hush-hush."

"So the Germans won't find out just what it is that they're laying around here?"

"Or maybe for some more intelligent reason, such as that perhaps we don't know ourselves."

"Don't you?"

"Whether or not we know would be another naval secret which Jerry would like to find out, wouldn't it? But there are certain things which everybody knows about explosive cutters. Think of a rather tiny mine—cheap to make and not big enough to dent a ship—but moored so that it will just touch our cutting cable when we are trawling for big ones. Whereupon it goes off with that loathsome little bump you felt when Bella started yipping, and snaps our cable. So we have to stop, sling out a new gear and later fish out the old one. Rather like finding toast crumbs in your bed, or snagging your last fly on the tip of a spruce tree when fishing for salmon in Scotland. You fish, I suppose?"

"Not a great deal any more."

"Hunt much?"

"Depending on what I've lost."

"Never lost a fox, by chance?" he inquired a little wistfully.

"Not that I remember."

"I'm sure you would if you had. Pity you haven't, because it's rather fun hunting them. Very little hunting these days, of course, with all the chaps at sea or with the army. Farmers are complaining the foxes are increasing so fast that—"

"But about explosive cutters—" I began.

"Think we had better talk about foxes," said the first officer firmly.

"Meaning you've told me all I should know about explosive cutters?"

"Perhaps," he said thoughtfully, "although there is one other little thing you might as well know—the fact that one of our boats will probably strike a whopper of a big mine in a minute. You see when Jerry lays a really big one, he usually protects it by planting a cute little bed of explosive cutters round it, hoping that they will cost us three or four cables and an hour or two in time before we can sweep up the big chap."

Our new gear has been slung over the side and we are under way again, with a new tin fish leaping through the water 200 yards out from our side. The grizzled old chief of staff with the shaggy eyebrows sniffs the fresh sea air like an old hunting dog.

"I say," he says, "I really am glad I decided to come. You've no idea how boring it is sitting at a desk. I hope I'm not in the way."

"It's an honor, sir," said the captain.

"I wonder if we shall meet anything today? Perhaps be dive-bombed? You know it's never happened to me. Perhaps if we are I shall be afraid." Here he chuckled shyly. "Wouldn't it be amusing if I were!" He walked over to the starboard side of the bridge to peer hopefully at *Deutsch Europa.*

"The old boy was in the last show," said the first officer to me in an awed undertone. "Has so many decorations for personal bravery he would look like the ribbon counter at Selfridge's if he ever wore 'em all."

Sweeping a given area of the trackless sea is much more difficult than cutting a field of wheat, so our captain is taking careful bearings, first on a distant lighthouse, then on a white chalk church spire. The driver of a combine tractor can tell to an inch just where he left off cutting the day before by looking at the stubble. But with no stubble to guide us, we must be just as accurate. How can a flotilla of mine-sweepers tell just where they swept the previous day? First they divide the sea into tracts on a chart, as a surveyor divides a rolling prairie into fields. A surveyor may mark the corners of his field with pegs. A mine-sweeper must locate the boundaries of his tract of water by constantly taking the most careful bearings. An error of a few hundred yards might leave unswept a mine field which would destroy a precious cargo ship.

The men who keep this channel clean insist their job is not very dangerous because, if properly handled, a mine-sweeper need almost never go into unswept water. The ship itself travels within the band swept the previous day. The cable and float project out into the danger area. But mine-sweeping is kept safe only by constant and careful navigation. The smallest mathematical mistake, or failure to allow for drift of wind and tide, brings great danger.

"How often does a trawler run nose onto a mine?" I ask.

The first officer grins. "Only once. That's the end of her."

"But how often does it happen?"

"That's a question we had better skip. Might be helpful to Jerry. He is a pretty careful reader of your American press."

"Aircraft off the starboard bow, sir!" calls the lookout. We rake the sky with our glasses and spot a black dot high, at least fifteen thousand feet, approaching us from *Deutsch Europa.*

"Think she is hostile, sir," calls the lookout in his singsong monotone.

The old chief of staff is peering up through his binoculars.

"It does look rather hostile, you know!" he says with a chuckle.

"It's the German spotter plane," the first officer explains to me. "Comes out regularly every afternoon to see what we are up to—maybe to take photographs. If there's a convoy moving through, it sends the bearing and range by wireless back to the German long range batteries around Calais. Now and then it dives down to rake a ship with machine-gun fire just for pure deviltry."

We can now hear the buzz of the plane's windscrew over our engine noises.

"I say, it does look hostile!" says the chief of staff eagerly.

The plane, now overhead, starts a big circle around us.

"She's unusually interested in us today," says the captain.

"Definitely hostile!" repeats the chief of staff with another boyish chuckle, following the plane with his glasses.

"We'd better look sharp—she may go into a dive," says the captain uneasily. Then, turning to the chief of staff, he asks, "Shall I signal for help, sir? We can have some Spitfires out here to chase her away."

"Oh, not on my account!" says the chief of staff. "Do just what you usually do. I only came out because one gets so tired of a desk ashore."

"We can easily get the Spitfires."

"Don't think of it," insisted the chief of staff, "unless it's what you usually do."

"Ordinarily we might not quite yet," says the captain.

Making a quiet mental note of the fact that I have not been asked if I feel the need of any Spitfires, I watch the plane complete her second circle. Now she straightens out and continues on toward the English coast.

The young first officer has filled his pipe.

"I say, may I borrow a light?" he asks.

I strike the match and he leans toward the flame. My hand wavers. It wavers because the entire bridge quivers like a plucked fiddle string. It quivers because the hull of the *Stella Orion* shakes as though a giant had suddenly pitched against her side an old-fashioned kitchen range with its fire-box, ovens and water reservoir solidly filled with lead—whereupon Bombproof Bella gives tongue in hysterical delight from the scuppers.

"I say, a mine!" says the first officer. "Look back there!" Back there, about a hundred yards out from the side of the second trawler, stands another of those slim ghostly columns of water—this one a little higher than the trawler's masts.

"Jolly close!" said the first officer excitedly. "Twenty yards nearer and it might have stove her in, and tossed the chaps on the bridge into the water. She must have had her cutting cable too near the surface so that it tangled in the mine's prongs. Or maybe Jerry has a new gadget to irk us."

"How many types of mines are there?" I ask.

"Must I take you fox hunting again?"

"But surely the Germans know how many kinds of mines they are laying?"

"Just as surely they'd like to know which types we understand and have learned how to render harmless, so they can abandon them and bring out some new models."

"Are the Germans so ingenious?"

"Occasionally. More often Jerry is a slavish creature of habit. Perhaps you've heard of Monday, Wednesday and Friday?"

"Some mention of them."

"It's a classic in all trawlers. Supposed to have happened up on the Thames Estuary. It seems this Jerry mine layer came out regularly every Monday, Wednesday and Friday night, to lay exactly the same number of mines in exactly the same places. Our chaps got onto this, so regularly every Tuesday, Thursday and Saturday morning they'd go out in a trawler and sweep them up. Went on for weeks, until finally our chaps got fed, and one Tuesday decided to skip a day to see what would happen. Just as they thought, the Jerry mine layer came out Wednesday night and promptly blew himself to bloody bits on one of the mines he had laid Monday. Our chaps got out there in a motor boat with a searchlight looking for survivors after the roar. Pulled in a dozen Jerries, including the captain. He was furious."

"At being outwitted?"

"Not at all. Wouldn't believe for a minute we had done it purposely. Very bitter at us for neglecting our duty in not sweeping up the field. Said such sloppiness would never be tolerated in the German Navy."

In the high blue skies above, another air battle is in progress. A Messerschmitt squadron flying in even formation leaves a trail like combed fleece threads. Into this dive Spitfires like the shuttles of a loom, breaking the even pattern into a tangled snarl as the planes pair off into dog-fights.

[191]

The opposing fighters have woven a shroud of death which floats lightly, bridging the channel skies. Just below its fabric I see three tiny yellow silver balls, no larger than peas hanging in the sky. They are parachutes of aviators who have bailed out—it will take them almost a half hour to fall from the high shroud of death into the cold Channel waters.

"Tea, sir?" A sailor is handing out thick china mugs of steaming hot tea, ready mixed with milk and sugar. Then a plate piled high with sandwiches, slabs of meat between bread slices generously hacked from the loaf by a man, not shaved by a woman.

Appetizers are the chill sea breeze which whips around us, the bright sun on the dancing water, the float which leaps through the waves alongside us like a dolphin; never was such a meal! We gulp great draughts of the steaming tea, gnaw off huge mouthfuls of the bread and meat, suck in deep bellyfuls of the pure air.

The old chief of staff is delighted. "So glad I came!" he explains. "It was really a sudden impulse of mine."

"Aircraft off the starboard bow, sir!" calls the lookout. "Think it's hostile." Instantly the gun crew rise and put on their helmets, standing beside their gun. There it is, flying low over the sea about five miles away—a sluggish black beetle.

The captain gazes at it and then hands his binoculars to the chief of staff. "It's only Grossmutter out on patrol,"

[192]

he explains. "She's a Dornier flying boat the Germans send over the channel to rescue their pilots who come down into the sea in parachutes. They claim she's a hospital plane—entitled to immunity like an ambulance. Of course we don't recognize any such claim." With his glasses he follows the fat old flying boat as she buzzes off toward the three parachutes—now close to the water. "Matter of fact though," he adds in a lower tone, "we have never yet fired on her."

"Hostile aircraft off the port beam, sir!" calls the lookout.

"It's the German spotter coming back," says the first officer. "She's altering course. Seems to be heading for us."

We fix her with our glasses. Not only has she changed course, but she is coming down rapidly.

"Shall I order action stations, sir?" asks the first officer.

"Not yet," says the captain. The plane grows from a black pinhead, to the size of a pea, to the size of a beetle. Without waiting for the order, the gun crew is standing around the breech of their gun, looking upward. I find that I am unconsciously measuring my distance from the steel railing. Now we hear the plane's airscrew—a venomous tearing buzz which drowns the lesser noises of our ship.

The old chief of staff chuckles delightedly. "What a hostile noise! Definitely hostile! I say, you chaps have no idea how nice it is to get away from one's desk!"

[193]

The buzzing black beetle is now a humming bird—quickly swells into a swooping crow. "Better order action stations," says the captain quietly. Then he turns to the old chief of staff. "Shan't I signal for the Spitfires, sir?"

"But they couldn't get up and out in time to be of much use, could they?"

"Possibly not."

"Then I certainly shouldn't. Seems a shame to bother them for nothing. Unless it's what you usually do." And now he turns to the plane which has grown to the size of an eagle. "Quite unmistakably hostile!" he chuckles.

"She's starting to dive, sir," shouts the first officer. And so she has—pivoting over on one wing, venomously coming straight down at us—the sun glinting on her black motor cowling like an angry eye. I move nearer the steel railing.

"I say, I wouldn't have missed this for anything," says the old chief of staff. But the captain is intent on the plane. "Better give her the first round now," he says.

The shouted command rings out, the ship shakes with the report, and a round black cloud appears midway between us and the plane. As suddenly as it dived, the plane now veers off. It is as though we had tossed a sack of soot in the eyes of an eagle. It swerves, levels, and as it twists into a climb, its wing bottoms catch the sun which is now low in the sky. It circles back overhead, now well out of range of our guns, then dwindles off toward *Deutsch*

[194]

Europa. I get up from behind the steel railing. The old chief of staff is beaming. "You know, I really shall do this more often. A little fresh air makes one almost feel like a boy again," he says with a shy chuckle.

A sailor climbs to the bridge with a folded paper. "Signal from number three ship, sir."

The captain reads. "They've brought a mine to the surface. We're just at the end of the day's run, so perhaps you'd like to watch them sink it."

He gives the order to turn to the wheelhouse below. I glance ahead at the empty horizon. Then I glance back to get the position of the other three ships. When I again turn my head, the ship has not had time to answer the helm, but the horizon ahead is no longer empty. About a mile ahead is what apparently is a waterspout, a hundred feet tall, and shaped like a snow-covered mountain spruce, motionless above the water. Except that it can't be a spruce or a waterspout. I pluck the first officer's sleeve and point.

"By Jove," he says, "they're shelling us! That filthy little spotting plane is trying to get her revenge. Must have been no end annoyed at our fire. She has sent in our position to the long-range batteries. That one was intended for us. Range isn't bad, but I must say the bearing is bloody awful—dropping at least a mile ahead of us."

We watch two more huge waterspouts suddenly rise, slowly fade into mist, and silently dissolve as our flotilla completes the big turn which points us back toward Dover.

All but number three ship, which stays motionless until the *Stella Orion* comes alongside, when we can hear the zipping chirrup of rifle bullets fired by an officer from her bridge, each one flicking a feather of spray from a wave. Among these bobs the shiny black round belly of the mine, a golf ball bigger than a washtub. The air-tearing chirrups of the rifle bullets continue.

The captain turns to the chief of staff. "Shall I order number three ship to move in closer, sir? They're firing at more than a hundred yards. May take them some time. At fifty they could sink it in three shots."

"Oh, don't think of it. They're quite close enough."

The red-headed first officer moves closer to me along the bridge railing. "Very decent old chap," he says in an undertone. "You see now and then the bullet, instead of puncturing and sinking the mine, explodes it. I've seen big mines open the seams of a trawler at a hundred yards. At fifty it might chuck the chaps off into the water. The old boy won't let anyone go into a dangerous position just to put on a show for him. Bloody good seaman he was, in his day. Had a command at Jutland and got decorated, although to hear him tell it you'd think he was never out from behind an Admiralty desk."

Our trawler and the other three little harvesters of death have reeled in their floats and tackle, and are now following the line of white cliffs back toward Dover. The mist trails of the afternoon air battles have thickened into huge ropes of fleece, the snarls fused into a single thin cloud bank which is blood red in the setting sun.

"You know I'd very much like to come out again," said the old chief of staff.

"Afraid you'll find it the same old grind, sir," said the captain. "Mine-sweeping is only exciting in the newspapers."

Perhaps. Only three days later I see at the bottom of a London evening paper a small item which chronicles the sinking in action of HMS trawler *Stella Orion*, and the rescue of all of her crew. And I am sure that, as her big blue-eyed captain was pulled grunting into the life boat, the reproachfully forgiving black eyes of unsinkable little Bombproof Bella were peeping out of his life jacket, just under his chin.

16. MARGARET: VI

WELL, poor little John has failed his tests. I wasn't there, but I saw the results. And they're pretty convincing, because they don't depend on how much you've been taught. It's purely a matter of how naturally smart you are.

In one, a simple triangle is printed in a large square at the edge of the paper. Beside it are a series of similar blank squares in which the kid is supposed to draw triangles exactly like the first. John filled in his first blank square with a pretty good imitation of the original triangle. But the second wasn't much like it. The third was barely a triangle, the fourth wasn't a triangle at all, and you couldn't tell at all what the fifth and sixth had ever started out to be. They were copies of copies of copies, and you could see the original image of the triangle had faded from poor little John's mind. But Margaret's triangles were still triangles, clear over to the edge of the paper.

Other tests were printed pictures in which something was missing, and the children had been asked to draw it

in. Margaret usually found it, but John only once. It was
the outline of a man who had only one arm. John had
drawn another on him—a pretty good arm, too—only it
came out of his knee.

"Maybe John was embarrassed," I put in, "because
Margaret was so much better than he. Maybe he was
afraid to try."

"Neither child," explained Hedy sadly, "could look at
the other one's paper, and I praised them both alike. John
seemed very relaxed and happy all through the test game.
And oh! so anxious to please! If only your wife could see
him! The world is full of clever people, but few so nice
as little John—I am sure she would want them both.
They love each other so much, and would be so happy
together!"

John wore my tin hat as he always does, for a minute,
before I hung it up. And then I went around with them,
as always, while they help Hedy do the blackout. John's
share is to push the buttons which turn on the lights. I
lift him up while Hedy lifts Margaret to do her share,
which is to pull the cord to close the heavy window curtains.

"Can they see any now?" asks Margaret.

"Pull it a little more."

"Can they see now?"

"Not now. Not even the smallest glimmer. You have
made the blackout very well." So it is, they tell me, every

night in every English home. Helping make the blackout has been added to the daily ritual of childhood.

Back in the nursery, busy with blocks, John builds a house for Margaret to bomb by dropping a big marble on it. Outside in the hall, Hedy explains sadly that John, who is five, tested only three. Not at all so well as Margaret, who is three-and-a-half years old. Margaret is a very unusual child, says Hedy, clever for her years.

I ask if there are a great many orphaned and homeless children in England due to the war. Hedy says the number has greatly increased, but there is no enormous surplus. Of course it frequently happens that when children are evacuated from London to the country, their parents, remaining in London, are killed by bombs. But such children are usually claimed by aunts or grandparents who can provide homes. There are not many, like John and Margaret, who have no near kin.

And then, Hedy says, the war has caused an increase in the number of people wanting to adopt children. They were childless couples living in towns out of London or in the country. When the government authorities, counting the surplus rooms in their homes, told them that three or four children evacuated from London would be quartered on them, at first they were horrified at the prospect. But when the children actually came, in a few months they began to dread the day when, after the war, they must go back to their real parents. They can't bear the house ever being so lonely and empty again, and thousands of such couples are trying to adopt children of their own.

And by the time my homeward-bound underground train has reached Marble Arch, I've decided what I'll do about the tests. Completely the hell with them, and with any future tests which might separate John and Margaret. Because brains are a dime a dozen in this blood-stained world, while freely-given, unasking love like little John's you find only a few times in a lifetime.

And who are you, White—to set any store by intelligence tests? What about those two years you spent trying to pass Algebra III in Emporia High School? And those Harvard oral examinations for divisionals you had to take twice before you could jerk your degree away from them? So you asked that these poor little children be tested, did you? All right, now you've got your tests and you know what you can do with them.

So now that is settled, and the only problem left is to arrange for transportation for John and Margaret to America. But first to cable Kathrine about the tests to see how she will react. It wouldn't be fair not to tell her what happened.

NLT WILLIAM WHITE CUMBERLAND HOTEL LONDON

DISREGARD TESTS CHILDREN SOUND LOVELY BRING BACK A WHOLE LITTER LOVE

KATHRINE

17 . LONDON FIRE

THE best way to tell any story is to start at the beginning. This one starts at a matinee of the Charlie Chaplin movie on a night the Nazis tried to burn London. I went to it with Marguerite, who is twenty-five and very good-looking. She is half English and half French and speaks both languages with just a trace of an accent. She used to work for *Le Matin* but got out of Paris just ahead of the Nazis and came to London where she now holds a newspaper job and on the side helps General De Gaulle's Free French forces with their publicity. Marguerite and I agreed that the Chaplin movie was good and in some parts of the world might be very, very good; but not hereabouts because, when you really know Nazis, nothing about them is very comical and some of the jokes were so true that they fell flat.

The show started at four thirty. At about the beginning of reel four we heard the air-raid sirens, and they flashed a notice on the screen that anyone who liked to could leave and go down into the shelter, which no one did. We were sitting in the front row center balcony. About fifteen minutes later we felt the entire balcony waggle back and forth, slowly and majestically, for about ten seconds, which meant a big one had dropped some distance away. Neither of us mentioned the waggling, but we knew that outside it must really be getting pretty hot. The show let out at seven o'clock and we stepped out into the weirdest city I had ever seen. Marguerite said that early in September, when the Nazis had burned the docks, it had been weirder but not much weirder. Anyway London looked like a production in technicolor of the burning of Rome by Cecil B. DeMille. The whole sky was pink, and in splotches around us on the horizon it was bright orange. It was so garish as to be a little bit overdramatized and in bad taste. Of course seven o'clock is long after dark, but there was enough light from this pink and orange sky for me to tell easily the tone of the lipstick Marguerite had slapped on, and she could make out that my suit was dark blue and not black.

We were going to have dinner, but first Marguerite had to drop by her office to check in on a story she had written that afternoon. The whole building was empty and we finally located the staff down in the basement with the presses and big rolls of paper. They were correcting proofs. They explained that the building was a rattletrap and they had been sent below until the stuff dropping thinned out a bit. She checked on the story, and then we started out to get something to eat. There were no taxis so we had to walk.

People along the streets were a little nervous, and sometimes someone would break into a trot or a run, when there was a good bomb whistle near by. Marguerite made a particular point of not running. Because of this crazy Cecil DeMille pink over everything, you could see the faces of the people, see which ones were scared and just how scared. A few of them weren't liking it at all.

There was so much pink in the sky by this time that we both knew this was already a big night for London and maybe was going to get bigger. So Marguerite suggested we walk over by the embankment to see just how big it already was—whether much stuff had dropped on the other side of the river.

When we got there we found the Thames was the same kind of baby ribbon pink as the sky, except for yellow flames from a barge that had caught fire, and high yellow flames in two patches from what might be warehouses. But most of the trouble was apparently on our side of the river. So then we started back to find a restaurant which might be open.

There wasn't a taxi in sight. Most of the people had cleared off the streets, except for policemen and air-raid wardens. Almost every vehicle we hailed turned out to be a fire engine, when it got close enough to see by that technicolor pink reflected from the sky. We wondered if we could read by it, so we took out our press passes and sure enough we could. And then all of a sudden stuff began bouncing all around us in the street—at first I thought it was shrapnel, but then each piece, as it struck, burst into a ball of greenish white flame about the size of a cat and the color of a mercury vapor lamp, and we knew they were incendiaries. Two of them landed within three yards and about half a dozen hit within ten yards. They were bouncing and rattling around all up and down the street. In the pink light now tinged with greenish white we could see the air-raid wardens running to put them out, and hear the watchers on the roofs above calling for help in dealing with those which had punctured tiles and gone through to rooms below.

Only it was those immediately around us, burning harmlessly on the sidewalk, which infuriated Marguerite's sense of tidiness. I turned around just in time to see her give one of those burning incendiary bombs a healthy kick which sent it spinning into the gutter. It had fallen close to a building on a square where glass ovals were set into the sidewalk. The glass on which this incendiary had rested was still bubbling. Marguerite was holding one foot in her hands and hopping around on the other. We took off her shoe. The leather was burned through, but the stocking beneath was only scorched, and she said it would probably raise only a small blister. She also said that anyway it was worth it.

So then we went across the street to a bank which had a lot of sandbags up around it protecting people's investments, and took half a dozen of these, one at a time, and dumped the contents over the rest of the burning incendiary bombs around us. The contents turned out to be ashes and clinkers instead of sand but it was almost as good.

On both sides of our street we could see roof fires starting. First there would be a curl of smoke above the eaves, then a flickering orange yellow glow would appear behind the top-story windows. Because this was the downtown commercial and financial district of London, most of the houses were vacant and there were few roof watchers. So the air-raid wardens in the street below had no way of knowing they were on fire until these lights appeared in the upper windows. Then I remembered something I had picked up in Berlin last fall a year ago and forgotten until just now. A Nazi newspaperman blowing off in front of a bunch of us after a foreign office press conference was bragging that large areas of London—the docks and the older parts of the city district—could be burned off like weed patches from the air any time they decided to do it.

So then Marguerite said that possibly this wasn't just a cute local fire but maybe a real story, possibly a big one which might take most of the night. I said in any case now was the best time to eat.

Everything in the neighborhood was closed but the Savoy, so finally we had to go to the Savoy. There was nobody in the big lobby but the attendants, who looked uneasy at what they knew was going on outside but of course were well-disciplined British servants. Down in the dining-room, which is one of London's most expensive restaurants and safest air-raid shelters, the people at the tables were well-dressed. Many of them were in uniform. They all had placid serene Munich-looking faces. The stuffy young correspondent of the pompous American paper who often dines politely with the elderly American-born peeress was dining politely with the elderly American-born peeress. Marguerite and I agreed on how easy it is to get very fond of the British people, who on the whole are so brave, and so truly courteous, and friendly, and tolerant, if you only stay out of the Savoy.

Across the room was a French officer in General De Gaulle's uniform whom Marguerite knew. She said he was one of the few who had enough money to eat at the Savoy, as most of the French who were able to get over here to keep on fighting got out of France with only the clothes on their backs.

I asked her about the French Navy, still under the control of Vichy, and she said that most of its officers came from narrow-minded reactionary petty-bourgeois families of Brittany, the old royalist stronghold, which had hated the revolution of 1789 and hadn't liked any of the subsequent ones any better. She said most of the officers of the French Navy were natural fascists whose only quarrel with Hitler was that he had the misfortune to be a German. In addition, she said, they were bitterly jealous of the British Navy because it was bigger, if Pétain gave the word to fight they would like nothing better, and the English had better keep all these facts in mind for future reference.

Then we went out in the street where the orange light was even brighter than before. There were no fires near us, but the glow was reflected up on a smoke and fog bank several thousand feet above by fires a quarter or half a mile away. We decided to take a taxi together if we could find one, but there seemed to be no taxis— only fire engines dashing through the empty streets which we could recognize blocks away by the reflected light from the smoke and fog bank. There were planes buzzing around in this, but only now and then were they dropping heavy stuff. The few people on the sidewalks were hurrying along, looking as if they didn't like any of it very well, which was only sensible.

Presently we heard the long, slow steadily rising whistle of a really big bomb coming down. We were in the middle of a block. Ahead of us were some soldiers who were about to cross the street at the intersection. When they heard the bomb coming they started to run. Just as they had reached the middle of the street the noise

had risen so loud and seemed so close that they threw
themselves flat on their faces, as soldiers are trained to
do when a shell comes over. This of course was the
wrong thing to do in London, where you avoid inter-
sections where the blast can hit you from any one of
four directions, but duck into doorways instead. But the
soldiers were obviously only on leave in London and
couldn't know this. However, nothing happened; the
bomb hit at least two hundred yards away, as we knew
by its long slow whistle that it would undoubtedly do.

Then suddenly we saw a taxi coming lickety-brindle
down the street away from the direction of the pinkest
glow in the sky. We hailed him and he pulled up. He
was a scared, rat-faced young man with flaring ears.
The hood of his taxi was splattered with drops of water
from fire hoses. He was very shaky and excitedly de-
manded which direction we wanted to go. We said we
wanted to go to the fire. He said he had just come
from there, and not for anything in the world would
he go back. He said the entire city was alight, out of
control, would burn to the ground tonight and he was
getting out. He was really badly scared. Then he said not
even for two quid would he go back, and waited to see
if we would offer him the two quid. But Marguerite said
this was too much, and besides she didn't want a frightened man around and we could probably find another

taxi or walk, and any way to say all of London would burn was childish nonsense. So we started out to walk.

About ten o'clock we finally found a taxi who would take us into the fire zone. He was a very nice, good-natured kid with a lot of thick black hair slicked down with grease. He said he would go because he would like very much to see it himself, and it would be whatever we thought it was worth. So Marguerite and I crawled into the back seat and we started towards the place where the sky was pinkest. The driver said he heard the flames were moving onto St. Paul's, and that the Guild House was going, and maybe would be gone before we got there.

We told him to drive for the reddest area of the sky ahead, and when he got into it, to try to steer for St. Paul's.

We rolled down the rear windows to hang out and watch the sky. Now and then we would pass a fire-engine pump puffing away at a hydrant, and our car would bump over a line of fire-hose running down the street and around a corner. But they led off to distant blocks and we saw no nozzles yet. We came to a rope barrier and there we first noticed the first smell of fire—just a whiff as we rounded a corner. The smell of a city fire is usually strong, rancid and just a little frightening. In it is often mingled the stench of rubber or the sourish odor of scorched tar roofing. There was none of these in this

smell. I remember noticing even then that for some reason it was vaguely pleasant and harmonized with the
orange glow which penetrated everything so that we
could see each other's faces even in the car.

Presently we came to a police line. Beyond it were
more fire engines and still beyond that, at the end of
the street, a yellow glare. The driver pulled up and we
held our press passes out through the window. The policeman touched his hand to the brim of his blue steel
helmet and waved us on through. This impressed the
driver greatly. He said he thought we were only a couple
of crazy sightseers and had not guessed we were reporters.
After that, every time we came to a police line he would
lean out and say, importantly, "We are the press" but
presently we found the street way blocked with fire engines, so we told the driver to park his car and we would
walk.

We were a little surprised to find that the fire was in
a building we both knew—a six-story affair which houses
a press association. The top story was ablaze and we could
tell the roof had fallen by the way the sparks rose. Firemen were playing about three feeble streams of water
from the street into the fifth story windows. The water
had knocked out the glass but they were still dark. Evidently they hoped to keep the fire from coming down
any lower by soaking the lower floors. We had both been
in that building half a dozen times, sitting on desks piled

with copy, talking to newspapermen we knew. It was silent now, and the bottom windows dark. There was only the hissing sound of the nozzles and the frying noise as the water hit the red hot roof timbers.

The firemen told us the worst fires were on down further into the city, and also they heard half a dozen churches were burning. So then Marguerite suggested we walk down a couple of blocks and over one, to see if her particular church was all right. She'd never been in it, but she passed it every day on her way to work, and it was a perfectly sweet little Christopher Wren church, nestled among some ratty old office buildings.

As we got near, it looked like a Christmas card picture of a church at night, a black silhouette with a holy light streaming from its windows. Only this light flickered uneasily. Someone, probably firemen at the beginning of the fire, had left the front doors open and light streamed out of here too. Standing as close to them as the heat would permit we looked into a great furnace. The roof had come down and broken chunks of its big glowing oak beams were sprawled over the red embers of the pews. From within the church came the steady rumble of a big hot fire at its peak, a noise which is deeper than a roar, but above this we could hear other sounds—clicking noises of falling and cracking rock. Then we saw what it was. The heat was peeling off pieces of the ancient stone sidewalls and pillars—chunks about the size of your hand and sometimes as big as your head, and there was almost a steady rain of these, in from various parts of the building, clicking and knocking and rattling down on the stone floor.

And here is what we thought as we watched this genuine old Christopher Wren church crumbling away in flames. First we thought how beautiful it looked in the shimmering heat. Then, being reporters, we thought what a good cable story it would make, because any church destroyed in a war gets a big play abroad. Then we thought that, after the war, people with too much money would give lavishly so that high-priced architects would restore it even better than it had been before the fire, and this money would be easy to raise. Then we thought that in the meantime its loss would make no great difference to the people living near by. Most of them belonged to other denominations anyway, and the congregations of these little Wren churches had in the past few decades been very small. And yet, as Marguerite pointed out, it was sad to stand here and see it go, because it had been such a sweet little soot-stained church with perfectly balanced classical lines, like a minuet in stone.

The smell of this fire was all around us now and Marguerite remarked how curious it was, not at all unpleasant but almost like incense or some very sophisticated perfume—rather a pity there wasn't some way to preserve such an odor. Because this wasn't the ordinary smell of fresh wood smoke. It was spiced with the odor of oak beams which had been put into places two hundred and fifty years ago, after the first great fire of the city of London. Tough, seasoned, mellowed old rafters and flooring hewn centuries ago, as well as the ancient records of venerable British business firms whose columns of figures supported the empire, were blended into the haunting odor we sniffed. Surely no attar of roses could ever be so expensive as this scent which you could only get by burning the city of London. It clung to our clothes and to Marguerite's hair as we walked on back to the car.

A wide detour now, and then we turn again toward the fires, in another attempt to reach St. Paul's. We go bouncing along a street down whose center trail hose-lines like giant strands of gray spaghetti. Now we must go cautiously with frequent stops, for these narrow streets are so traffic-congested that often we can barely crawl. And it's a traffic jam the like of which I hope you will never see again in this generation. For, with the exception of our car, all of it was fire engines—hose carts, pumps, hook and ladder wagons—slowly oozing into the fire zone ahead.

Then we turned into an alley where we could leave the car. The kindly, courteous British police didn't tell us to. Our press passes would have carried that car further in that slowly moving stream, but our consciences got the better of us. If we continued on foot, at least

we wouldn't add to the traffic jam. The driver asks if
he may come with us. He explains he has never seen
anything like it, and maybe never will in his life again,
and do we mind? We say of course he may. So he follows along, keeping deferentially about two paces behind us. We explain that if we are stopped by police,
Marguerite and I will produce our passes, while he fumbles in his pockets and the three of us can probably walk
through.

The minute we get out, we notice the high wind which
snaps Marguerite's skirts, picks up bits of paper in a
mad dance and makes me hold my felt hat firmly on my
head. I hadn't bothered to take my steel helmet to a
movie matinee. Has this wind come up suddenly? We
didn't notice it a few blocks back.

We turn into the Cathedral square and see that the
great church itself is so far safe. We can see the tiny
outlines of its roof watchers just below the dome. But
the street behind it is in high twisting flames, and the
row of buildings on the right may break out at any
minute. The fire is already at their backs and, while
their fronts facing the Cathedral are still dark, light glows
ominously from an occasional window. In front of them
are three tall ladder wagons, and from the top of each
ladder a fireman is playing a stream of water into the
high dark windows. Obviously they are trying to hold

a water barricade here to keep the fire behind from sweeping on over the Cathedral.

Walking under these four- and five-story ladders, stepping over writhing lines of fire-hose, we go around to the back for a look at the burning street behind. Here again the firemen are trying to hold the blaze to the rear of the buildings. But two are already in flames and more are smoldering.

This is a shabby business district, and we are standing in front of a little jewelry store, surprised to see a light turned on. But it's not that—it's only the fire which has just broken through a hole in the upper left-hand corner of the room; a tiny, white inquisitive tongue of flame sticks out, lights the room like a dim electric bulb. As we watch, another bit of plaster falls, and another white tongue follows it. And then another—the room is much brighter now. We watch the little tongues appear until there are a half dozen—until the entire back wall is a flickering mass and the silver- and gold-plated stuff in the show-cases glitters in the wavering light. It is a poor little shop, with the sad jewels which the poor can afford, and then only rarely. But there are wedding rings in the window which soldiers give their girls, and pigskin picture frames which the girls buy to frame the pictures of their soldiers.

Now we see something curious happening in the show-cases. Here and there comes a sudden small burst of very

pure white light which quickly dies down again. It must
be very hot in the little shop, now that the back wall is
aflame. Perhaps these are jewels exploding. The room is
now filling with smoke but even through this we can
see the white will-o'-the-wisps dancing on the counters.
More likely it is not jewels, for pearls, even if they were
real, would only char. It is the celluloid in cheap comb-
and-brush sets which leaps suddenly into these pure white
balls of flame.

In the display window the straps of the cheap wrist
watches are beginning to writhe like little snakes in the
heat, and the pigskin on the picture frames is cracking
and curling. Where is the little man who owns this shop?
What will he do tomorrow when he sees it? Maybe we
could break a window and save a little of his precious
tawdry stock for him even now. But how would we know
what was valuable, or how would we ever find the little
man? So we stand there in the empty street and watch
the glass show-cases crack, and the pigskin of the picture
frames curl, and the poor little wedding rings melt in
the growing heat. It seems so much sadder than the
Christopher Wren church, because no prosperous and
pious people will get a spiritual uplift out of rebuilding
this little jewelry shop with loving care exactly as it was.
In fact, nobody will know or care that it is gone, except
the poor little owner and his shabby customers, who
scrape up a few shillings and come in to buy some glit-

tering bit of metal, or tiny sparkling stone, to commemo-
rate a birthday or a wedding, or some other pathetic
milestone in the short and simple annals of the poor.

Further down, the street opens into a little square, and
we cross to the other side where people are streaming
out of a cellar. They are very tired and very poor. Air-
raid wardens are helping them carry bundles of bedding.
They stand on the sidewalk bewildered. They tell Marguerite that first they were in a shelter a quarter of a
mile walk from here. But presently wardens told them
the building above was aflame, and they must pick up
their dirty quilts and battered pillows and move to another. They had been there only an hour when the wardens came again and said the fire was moving closer,
and they must move. They were walked several blocks,
and finally found space for their mattresses in an already
crowded shelter, when again the wardens told them that
the fires were moving onward. Where were they being
taken now? The wardens hadn't told them. Maybe no
one knew yet. Anyway they were standing in a line on
the sidewalk—poor people, janitors and charwomen and
others who live in this financial district because they
must sweep and clean its offices—coming up out of the
cellar to stand bewildered, holding their ragged bedding.

Yet there was no grumbling and no hysteria. The wardens were good sturdy Londoners, tired with work and

responsibility, but with those steady British nerves we had been watching all evening. And, always, that unfailing, even, kindly, British politeness with which these people can smooth over the rough edges of even the worst crisis. Again we agreed that if you only stayed out of the Savoy it was so easy to see they were a fine, brave, kindly and noble people. After all, it isn't hard to stay out of the Savoy.

We crossed the square and walked down a winding street, again toward the pinkest part of the glare in the sky over the horizon chimney pots, picking our way over a dozen or more fire-hoses which ran down the street. And presently we noticed another steady wind, blowing down the street past us into the pink glare ahead. A hundred feet more, round a bend in the street, we come on a double rank of fire fighters, lined up with their backs to us, looking down the street at an upside down Niagara of flames. We could tell they had been brought in from distant boroughs of London by the insignia on their collars. We showed our press passes and they let us through, although they shook their heads dubiously at letting Marguerite pass, and warned us to look out sharply for falling bricks. So we walked down into the flaming street.

Meanwhile the breeze had risen to a March gale. Marguerite's red-golden hair streamed straight out in front of her forehead, her skirts whipped and snapped in front of her knees, and I held my hat on my head with one hand. A few blocks back there had been no breeze at all. This was a torrential river of cool air rushing down this narrow street to fill the vacuum left by the thousands of cubic feet of hot air which, each minute, were being hurled high into the sky by the flames of this burning block of buildings. The fire roared like a thousand great chimneys, as loud as the roar of air behind the propellers of a loaded bomber about to take off. It had created its own draft.

For a minute we stood and watched it at the head of the street. The shop fronts in this block were narrow —about twenty-five feet wide—and the buildings about six or seven stories high. Relentlessly the fire was moving toward us. The heat from one burning building would burn out a partition that separated it from its neighbor. Presently the wooden floors would crash down, the roof come tumbling in and the narrow building would be transformed into a five-story chimney with a roaring pile of debris piled at the bottom. Then the fire would be hot enough to move into the next building, and it was taking not more than two minutes to go from one twenty-five-foot shop front to the next. Above the deep rumble of flames we could hear another steady noise—a curious, even patter not unlike the fall of raindrops with a jingling clink. It was glass from the roasting window casements of all these little shops and the flats above them—as the heat of the advancing flames cracked the panes, or burned away the woodwork, the glass was tinkling down on the sidewalk in a steady musical drizzle.

I remember the days back in the wheat belt when, after a dangerously long spring drought, the farmers would stand out in the barn lot, and raise the palms of their hands to feel the first few big drops come pounding down, and as they heard it grow to a rumble on the tin roof, would say, "Oh, boy, it's a million dollar rain!"

Looking on down the flaming street, you could see the shop fronts which had caught alight some time ago, now burned out to mere shells of brick, and sometimes these would collapse in the dull red heat. There would be a clicking rumble as a store-front crumbled and came down in an avalanche of bouncing red-hot bricks, over the sidewalk, and out beyond the middle of the street.

The draught and fire rose in a high red column of sparks, but presently it curved over, and we could see that at the very end of the street, the heaviest sparks were descending in a shower against the blackness of a tiny darkened square in which was a little church. And this was the most beautiful thing I have ever seen, because it was a slow fall of fiery snowflakes—enormous ones coming gently and gracefully down in lovely curving spirals.

We were already dangerously far down into that burning street. Behind us I could see the firemen were watching us uneasily. But I knew they were really looking at

Marguerite. And a part of the picture of this whole fantastic night is the fact that Marguerite is a strikingly handsome girl. She was without a hat, and all that curly red-gold hair was being blown about by the fire draught. She was wearing tweeds and blue wool stockings and low-heeled shoes. Few men realize that one of the pleasant things about being out with Marguerite is that other men always turn to look at her—admiringly, of course, but always with respect. She isn't the kind of girl that an Italian would whistle at, but even a Swede would turn around to look. Something in her carriage shows she is also brave.

Now bravery in a woman counts for nothing in America, and for very little in a man. It's a quality which in time of peace you may not need once in a lifetime. A knowledge of shorthand is infinitely more useful. But war changes this and bravery—real steady courage—becomes the nicest quality which any man or woman can have, and people who don't have it suddenly don't count. I don't know why. I only know that cowards suddenly cease to exist as people and their opinions on any subjects are of no consequence whatever. Perhaps after the war this will change back. I hope so, because some of the cowards I used to know were very clever cowards, and their opinions seemed to be well-documented.

The firemen were looking at Marguerite, but Marguerite was looking down the flaming street into that beautiful snowstorm of sparks. "But it's magnificent," said Marguerite. "It's Wagnerian! It's a blizzard of fire! I want to run through it."

"It's not sensible," I said.

"It's not sensible to be a fireman," said Marguerite. "It's not sensible to be out at all tonight. It's not even sensible for less than fifty million English to be fighting almost a hundred million Nazis. All the sensible people in London are down under the Savoy Hotel."

"It's much more beautiful looking at it from here, than it will be when we get down in it," I said.

"Probably," said Marguerite. "Almost everything is more beautiful from a safe distance. Only I've got to find out for myself. Are you coming?"

"Yes," I said. And then I said to the driver, "You wait here and we will come back around the block and meet you at the car."

"I'm coming with you," said the driver suddenly. He didn't say "sir" and we were both glad he didn't.

"Why?" I asked.

"For the same reason that you are," said the driver. "This is my town, and this will never happen again, and I don't want to miss any of it."

So we started running down that flaming street. I put Marguerite on the side of me opposite the crackling buildings and took hold of her arm to steady her as we ran over the occasional piles of hot bricks. The driver, instead of walking respectfully two paces behind us, came up and took her other arm. He was a damned good, brave, steady, self-respecting British boy, and we both liked him very much.

The fire was terribly hot. I could feel it roasting the oil out of my right cheek and I turned up the collar of my trench coat, and with my free hand turned up the collar of Marguerite's tweed coat. The driver turned it up on his side. He was looking after her too. It got hotter and hotter as we ran, and the burned-out shop doors were like the openings into blast furnaces. It was a deep shimmering bluish red inside but it hurt you to look at it. A few sparks began coming down. They were bits of burning, charred wood about the size of your thumb nail which had been sucked up high in the air by the blast, and were now settling back. I had to brush them quickly off the shoulders of my trench coat, and off Marguerite's tweed coat, or they would have burned big holes in the cloth. It was not fun doing this, and squinting your eyes against the heat, and running over tumbled hot bricks.

All at once there was a crackling, clicking sound behind us which swelled into a clattering roar. We glanced back to see that the entire five-story front of the building we had just passed had collapsed in an avalanche of red-hot bricks and flaming timbers into the street. A sloping mass, which was piled several feet deep over both sidewalks. Now we knew we could never get back, but must go on, down the flaming street into the blizzard of fiery snowflakes before another building collapsed in front of us and trapped us between. As we ran we could hear the firemen shouting. I don't know what they were saying. But the only sensible thing they could have said was to keep on running as we were.

Then we passed the last burning building, and came out into the darkness of the little square, where the big sparks were showering down. But we could hardly see them. Because coming down with the sparks was choking acrid smoke that burned our eyeballs and made tears stream out. The sparks were so thick I was afraid Marguerite's hair would catch fire, so I clapped my felt hat on her head. The sparks kept coming down on my bald spot, and I kept brushing them away. The smoke almost strangled us. Both Marguerite's eyes were closed and so were the driver's. I had one eye which I could keep open by propping it with my forefinger and thumb, so I put my arms around both of their waists and led them across the square, telling them to step up, when we came to gutters and curbs.

Then we found a dark street where there was no fire, and presently we found our way back to the car. It was four o'clock in the morning, and Marguerite decided she had better go home, as she had to get to work at seven-thirty. No one said anything as we took her home. After about fifteen minutes we looked back. The burning city of London was now only a tall column of orange, surrounded by a technicolor pink aura on the horizon behind us through the car window.

"Wasn't it beautiful and weren't the people nice?" said Marguerite.

"I never knew nicer people."

"Nice, and clean, and brave, and steady, and beautiful people," said Marguerite, "and now I want to go to sleep."

So we took her home, and then the driver took me home, and when I paid him he said quite solemnly that he wouldn't have missed it for anything. And he didn't say "sir."

Next day I had a close-up glimpse of British morale. Of course everybody in America knows it is wonderful. Particularly those people back home who are aiding Britain by wearing little enameled buttons. They ask you isn't it too marvelous that the British are so magnificent, so everything is now just duckie and we can go back to our bridge game.

Well, I spent the day climbing over rubble in the choked streets of the charred City district of London—all that is left of the recent fire, in company of Bill Vandivert of *Life* magazine who was taking pictures.

We had found the whole district roped off and behind police lines.

The place had been magnificently beautiful the night of the fire. By the dull winter daylight it was a shambles, almost deserted except for occasional firemen playing hoses on heaps of rubbish. But once we ran into half a dozen neatly dressed businessmen in well-brushed bowler hats, the directors of a famous London bank. They had trudged through the rubble to peer, over a shattered wall, at a safe which contained the company's records. It had crashed through to the basement and now lay on its side —a steel island in a pool of charcoal-stained water.

We met another young man who said his business had been bombed out twice before and recently he had moved it down here. Today he got permission to pass the lines and climb through several blocks of rubbish to see if anything was left of it. Nothing was.

Presently we happened onto a couple of elderly men, partners in some firm which had been completely destroyed. They were asking their way, because some of the streets they couldn't recognize. When they discovered we were American reporters, they began talking as people often do when they realize they may be quoted.

"We will carry on," one of them said, "no doubt about it, in spite of things like this. Our spirit isn't broken. After all, what else is there to do? Carry on! That's what we should do!"

They said these things half to themselves, half to us, because they knew we were reporters. We turned off at a side street and left them climbing over rubbish toward their little business, which both we and they knew they would not find.

In a street as deserted and ruined as any in Pompeii we met three cockney firemen, playing a hose on a smoldering basement. They were astonished that we should be Americans, and very glad.

"Funny, running onto you chaps from so many miles away," the youngest said.

"Tell me," said the middle-aged one, "what does America think of all this?"

So we said something about America's sympathies being all with England.

"How soon do you think America will be in this?" asked the oldest fireman.

We had to say we didn't know.

"Do you think by spring?" he asked.

We had to say we didn't know.

"Maybe at least by summer?"

We had to say we didn't know.

"How long do you think this war will last?" asked the middle-aged fireman. He was very tired, having had almost no sleep since the big raid Sunday night, and his face showed it. We had to say we didn't know. The youngest fireman said he thought it might last four or five years.

"It can't last that long," said the oldest fireman. "This

sort of thing didn't happen in the last war. This one is going much faster than the other. I don't see how anyone can stand it more than a year or two." He told us he had been in the army all four years of the last war.

All day people we met in the district would ask us if we had seen the King. A rumor was going round that he was coming down here, as he frequently does, to devastated districts.

The young King has no vivid personality, but the English people, after a disaster, are most eager to see him. His appearance is for them a symbol that the rest of the nation is in touch with them, appreciates their bravery and will help.

So all day in that shattered city with jagged soot-stained walls, people asked us if we had seen the King and what we thought America would do. We hadn't seen the King and we didn't know about America.

18. MARGARET: VII

I'VE just made a discovery. I had decided, regardless of tests, to take them both back to America, but today I find that it will be absolutely and completely impossible to get space for even one extra person on the Imperial Airways plane which connects at Lisbon with American boats and clippers. This plane (it goes only twice a week and holds only eight people) is England's only link with the continent. Americans have been waiting months for places on it, and my own single reservation has just been postponed another two weeks. Completely useless even to ask for another seat even for one child, when weight is so carefully counted that I must cut even my baggage down to 40 pounds—but now wait! Have I got something here? Because last night on the bathroom scales Margaret weighed exactly 32 pounds and John 37!

Maybe the idea is crazy, but Gwen Barker won't think so. She's an executive assistant up in the Ministry of Information, and when I arrived here from Finland last year I then made the discovery that she's the most completely and selflessly helpful person in these islands, and can cut more red tape and get more done for you with that cool, gentle, persistent voice of hers over the telephone in five minutes than any two cabinet ministers.

Gwen Barker won't think it's crazy if I want to take a child out of here instead of my baggage, which I can cut down to a single pair of pyjamas and a toothbrush. Of course it's irregular, but if anyone can arrange it, she can.

Gwen Barker has come through! The Air Ministry finally agrees with her that I may take a child on the plane in lieu of baggage, provided the child sits on my lap and does not occupy a seat. And I wonder how many precious hours of her inexhaustible tact it took—her cool, sympathetic voice soothing this brass hat's rumpled dignity and building up that one's sense of importance. And I wish more Americans could come over here and see, behind the glittering British façade of lions and unicorns and medieval gew-gaws, through to the kindly, intelligent, gentle people like Gwen Barker, working desperately hard to keep her country free. They are the ones who keep this show going and will in the end produce the victory.

In all this there is only one consolation; thank God I don't have to choose between the children; the tests at least did that for me. It will be Margaret who will come to America and little John who must stay here.

Since little John must for the present go back to Mrs. Swope, the sooner he goes the kinder it will be to him, Hedy insists.

Because immediately she must start preparing Margaret for the idea of the trip to America with me. And how terribly it would hurt little John if he had to understand that I, whom he has come to love so much, was taking Margaret and leaving him behind.

And also Margaret must never know that it was I who took John away. Because, since she is so fond of John, she could not understand why I had done it and might come to fear or hate me. So it is arranged that Margaret shall not know that it is I who am coming for John tomorrow. But really, for John's sake, it should be I who take him. Because it was I who brought him, and it would be a terrible hurt if he were to think he has to leave here because people do not love him. He must not feel rejected.

Next day, when my taxi drew up in front of 13 Wedderburn Road, poor little John, in his tight-fitting English schoolboy's cap and his blue overcoat, one of his hands holding tightly to Hedy's, comes sadly, unwillingly but obediently down, step after step, to the sidewalk. He is clutching to his breast the shabby dirty little stuffed lamb which he brought with him when he came.

Where is the beautiful, expensive chartreuse teddy bear which I gave him for Christmas, and which he has always slept with since? Hedy explains in whispers. She hadn't exactly told John he would never see Margaret or the kindergarten again, but she is sure he has guessed it. When she gathered together his clothes and told him to pick out the toys he liked best, he had cried bitterly and insisted that all the toys should stay. Maybe because, if he left the things he loved, this kept the parting from being final. Then he could hope he might come back.

But why did he take with him the poor old dirty, woolly lamb, with only one bead eye? He had had it so long he was tired of it, and yet maybe he took only this because it was a part of him. Or maybe because it was such a sad, shabby little lamb that he feared no one else would ever love it, or be good to it, or see that it got properly put to bed at night.

When the taxi starts I lift him on my lap but he does not look at me, or talk at all, or count the bomb craters. He only stares out of the window. He has become shy again. He is being taken by someone who is supposed to like him (only do I really?) from a place which he loved so much and where people seemed to love him (only did they really?) back to someone he calls Mummy Swope who says she wants him to come back because she loves him so much (only does she really?).

The taxi swerves around bomb craters, it passes fascinatingly jagged walls of shattered houses, but little John

[233]

stares at the taxi floor, lost in that sad protective silence of a child which we call shyness.

Everything is arranged for the trip back to America, Margaret's passport and quota visa signed and sealed, except that now she can't stand the sight of me. It began the day John left. Whenever I come in the room she looks at me mistrustfully and, raising her hand, strikes out in the air as though to waft me away.

And Hedy says it's because she doesn't want to leave Anna Freud's kindergarten. Hedy tries to explain to her what a nice place America is, and that no little children can stay long at the Rest Center. And Margaret tries to understand it. But she doesn't want to go away—even with me whom she used to like. And maybe she guesses it was I who took John away. She might have heard my voice outside the house the morning John left. Anyway I am now the man who takes little children away, she strikes out and even starts to cry when I appear and I'm faced with the gloomy prospect of crossing the Atlantic with a three-and-a-half-year-old girl who can't stand the sight of me.

19. RECESSIONAL

"AND here are Margaret's things," says Hedy. Margaret, holding Hedy's hand tightly, looks around my hotel room with sad listlessness, at me with hopeless distaste.

"—her toothbrush," continues Hedy cheerfully, "and her duckie." And of course her incendiary bomb. It fell in her garden without going off, and next day the block air-raid warden unscrewed the magnesium case, emptied the thermite (it looked like corn meal) into the dirt and gave the now harmless bomb to Margaret. It's her most prized possession; it now weighs less than a pound and surely I can find room? "And also a pencil," concludes Hedy, "so Margaret can write a letter to me."

Margaret begins to sob.

"Mr. White will help you," Hedy soothes. "You can write from America."

Margaret doesn't want to sit on my lap in the taxi. She is resigned to the trip, but not to me. People turn around to look twice, as we walk along the station platform. I concede we were an odd pair—me in my old trench coat stained black with trench dirt and streaked white with salt water, a tin hat bouncing up and down on my left buttock, my Leica and binoculars in their leather cases dangling from my neck—my down sleeping bag and inflatable rubber mattress done up in a roll in the rucksack on my back (there are no porters) and in my right paw the tiny mittened hand of a little girl in red leggings and a pixie hood.

In the railway carriage, I start to sit down beside her.

"Don't sit there!" she orders.

So I start to sit down opposite.

"Not there!" I get up. "Over there," and she waves me to the far seat on the other side of the train. Anything to keep the peace. I pretend to read. I feel very foolish, cowed and blackmailed.

What the hell are you, White? A man, or a soft punching bag for hysterical women of all ages? Who's running this show, anyway? Very firmly I move over.

"I don't like you near me," shouts Margaret.

"What do I care what you like? If you don't like it, go over to the other side yourself."

She gets up to see if I really mean it. She moves down to the far seat, her eyes never leaving my face. She stares at me, perplexed, but thinking hard, trying to figure out this revolution. I look out of the window. It's the soft English countryside, green even in winter.

We stop at a station. It can't quite yet be our station. Maybe I can ask someone on the platform. As I step out a sudden scream of fright stabs me. Margaret comes running toward me, her eyes wide with terror.

I pick her up. "What's the matter, darling? Did you think I was going to leave you?"

She nods solemnly.

"Daddy won't ever leave you, not ever. Now let's sit down here and look out of the window." The gray clouds hang low as we pull out of the little station. But she can't look. She is fighting hard, but the little chest is heaving. As sudden as a summer shower, tears gush from the black eyes. She buries her head in the collar of my trench coat.

"That's all right," I say, patting her back softly, "go ahead and cry."

She is asleep as we rumble on through the darkness, a blacked-out train roaring through a blacked-out countryside, not a single ray of light glimmering from any cottage window now that the bombers range the high skies. A strange feeling comes over me—I definitely do not want to be killed. It began about a week ago.

Often when I have been in noisy, tight places the idea has occurred to me that it would be pleasant to survive, but I stayed because there were things I wanted to watch, or a job to be done. The chance of being killed seemed not enormously to matter.

But my work is over. I am trying to get home. All week

I hadn't liked it when the stuff came sizzling down. I was headed home. I wanted to get out alive.

Above all, on this home-bound train I don't want Margaret killed. For the moment I am brazenly unheroic. All I ask of life is a little more of it, and to get Margaret out of this damned, brave, bomb-churned, quivering country.

The Royal Bath Hotel at —— is like any one of a dozen big summer hotels built in the 1890s along the coasts of Maine and of England. The room-clerk is a brisk, middle-aged woman.

"You're Mr. White? We are very sorry to tell you the flight's been canceled. Weather, we think."

"When do we go?"

"Perhaps tomorrow."

I pick up Margaret and follow the boy with the bags.

Tomorrow proves a gray chill day with breakers floundering over the flat packed sand, gulls wheeling and screeching.

"That's the sea. We'll go down close so you can run on the sand of the beach."

Not so easy. The road is barricaded with slabs of concrete against tanks. Barbed wire has been woven around these, leaving a passage just wide enough for one person to squeeze through.

Huge coils of barbed wire, breast high to me, are piled along high tide mark. Beyond stretch the now empty beaches. Every hundred yards there are bath houses piled high with sandbags, roofs removed, machine-guns' snouts showing. We can't get down onto the sand. Up on the cliffs are more sandbagged gun nests.

There is no opening in the tight-woven barbed wire, so we walk up to High Street to do some shopping. Even a war correspondent, when he's been with a child for a few days, begins to notice what the other kids are wearing. Margaret's little red outfit with the peaked hood had seemed cute at first. Now I see that it is badly worn, much too small and there are holes in the soles of her shoes.

In the infant's wear section of the department store, Margaret knows exactly what she wants. That blue coat, with matching hat and leggings—definitely not the green one. But while I get my change, Margaret runs to another show-case.

"Babar!" she cries.

And so it is, a little stuffed elephant, blue with pink linings to his ears, exactly as he looked in the pictures of the book I had read to her and John every night.

Never after this is she quite so lonely. Because Babar has his tea with us—I tie a napkin on him. When Margaret has cornflakes, Babar has a spoonful. And a sip of her milk. And at bedtime he also has his bath—not a real one which would make his colors run, but a p'tend bath —the sponge squeezed until it is only damp, and then Margaret dries him on her towel.

Last night, because she had no other toys, she took the empty incendiary bomb to bed with her. But tonight it is Babar, who also must be kissed and tucked in.

"And you have the bomb. I give it to you for yourself."

"Margaret, I don't need the bomb."

Her face falls. "I *want* you to." She likes Babar best, and yet she can't bear to think of the poor rejected bomb, sitting on the dresser, not in bed with anybody.

In the middle of the night I wake, dreaming someone pokes a gun in my ribs. I have rolled over on that damned bomb.

We get into the car lit by the doorman's torch. The passengers are all men—sleepy, grumpy, in thick overcoats, uncomfortably squeezed into this tiny British car. Out in the bay, a mile away, we can see our plane. Then England falls away behind our motor launch and the plane looms big.

We're in. My safety belt is buckled tightly. A roar of motors, a few gentle bumps and we are away.

They let me crawl back to the luggage compartment to get Margaret's bib out of the rucksack, and she does pretty well by a couple of thin chicken sandwiches, a glass of milk and three stewed figs.

The climbing sun has dissolved the surface haze, so we climb too, up to about 5,000. But the air is pretty bumpy and some of the passengers are pale around the gills. Margaret seems not to notice that some of the passengers are fumbling for paper bags. Our heartiest traveler is the ruddy-faced Englishman—Sir Somebody Something-or-other—immaculately tailored.

Sir Somebody is eager for information about our country and its state of mind. His questions were tactful, and completely unpatronizing and he dandles Margaret on his knee to which she politely submits, eyeing me constantly.

Presently the long blue coastline of Portugal comes in view.

Our floats splash down in the great Lisbon harbor. We board the launch which takes us to the customs' house.

At the Avenida Palace Hotel, where I cabled for reservations a week ago:

"Yes, Mr. White, we received your cable. But," reproachfully, "that was last week."

We inspect three, each successively more tawdry, hotels —are full. The fourth is down by the waterfront, the Hotel Hamburg. They have rooms. There is no question of looking further. Margaret must get settled for the night.

The circles under her eyes getting bigger and darker every minute as she stands there holding my forefinger trustingly in one little hand and clasping Babar by his nose in the other—I haven't the heart to look further.

We'll have to use the public bathroom on the fourth

floor. There is no running water in the dingy room with its high windows—one huge double bed in one corner, and a collection of porcelain basins, water jugs and slop bowls, plus a peculiarly Latin contraption, a little white oval vessel squatting conveniently low on spindly legs. Margaret immediately spies it with delight.

"Look! a bathtub—just for Babar!" But then comes another problem. "Daddy—you take me to the lava'tory. I want to go."

I've already seen them down the hall, and here is your problem, Mrs. Post: a forty-year-old war correspondent escorting a three-and-a-half-year-old girl on a matter of some urgency in Portugal; which door do we enter? I shrink from fluttering the Portuguese dove-cotes behind the one marked "Senhoras," so we enter the side marked "Homines." Here is a fantastically variegated display of Latin plumbing fixtures in various stages of leakage and disrepair, one of them occupying the attention of a stout Portuguese military man with handlebar mustaches. He glances over his shoulder at Margaret, leaps like a startled fawn, wildly adjusts his garments, retreats fuming from the room with an indignant jingle of tunic medals.

"Daddy, who was that funny man?"

"A Portuguese Colonel of Coast Artillery, Margaret."

"What did he say to you?"

"I don't know, darling. He said it in Portuguese."

"Daddy."

"Yes, Margaret."

"Why don't they have a chain to pull like at Hedy's?"

"Because they have a button you can push, like in America."

"I want to go to Merika today."

As we leave the dining room after dinner we pass the hotel entrance doors and Margaret hangs back, pointing.

"Oh, daddy, look!"

I turn my head to see that she is staring, transfixed with delight. Suddenly I realize that Margaret has never before seen street-lights or neon signs. England has been blacked out since she was a year and a half old.

"They're street-lights, darling."

"Why do they have them?"

"Street-lights are every place where there isn't any war. They don't have any war in Lisbon."

"Why do they have a war in England?"

After she is asleep that evening I tiptoe out to do a little reporting, and I take my beer standing up at the Avenida Palace bar in Lisbon, and look over the crowd at the tables. Waiting for an old friend—an American reporter now stationed permanently in Lisbon. Of course the place is crawling with Gestapo. I'm used to that. I watched them busy as beavers in all the Grand Hotels of Europe last year from Stockholm to Bucharest. There are duller

[243]

forms of entertainment for a wandering journalist than to let himself be picked up by one of the heavy-handed spies the Nazis assign to bars, and watch them strain and sweat to pump out a few items of unimportant information.

Scanning the crowd I hope that at least a fair share of the weather-beaten sirens and alert young men with carnation boutonnières are working for the British. Last year in Scandinavia, just before the invasion, they were inadequately represented by engaging young idealists sent out by the British Council to give lectures on the architecture of seventeeth century London, illustrated by lantern slides, which they carried in leather cases. In retrospect, tommy-guns would have been more practical.

I am presently engaged in idle talk by a swarthy young man standing next me who has just ordered a Haig and plain water. His English has an American accent—with a trace of something else. He says he was five years in the oil business in Texas, now is in business in Lisbon, but offers nothing else about himself. I volunteer the fact (there can be no harm in it) that I have just come from England by plane, and expect to be returning to the States tomorrow.

Did I come by land plane or seaplane? Well, there is no harm in telling this anonymous young businessman that I arrived in a seaplane which settled down in Lisbon harbor yesterday in plain view of every spy.

"Too bad you didn't come by land plane from Bristol—then you could have seen Lisbon's airport," said the young man casually. "Lots of amusing things happen out there. You see, the British Imperial Airways land planes come in twice a week from England, and the Deutsche Lufthansa passenger planes run their regular service down from Berlin. Last week I myself ran into an amusing incident there. All the big oil companies have gasoline pumps at the airport, and I happened to be talking to an American friend of mine who has charge of the pumps of a big American oil company there.

"We were interrupted in our chat when one of the Lufthansa planes came taxiing over to this American pump, and asked to be filled up with high octane gas. He asked for a particular grade which could be used in a transport plane. Or it would be even more useful in a fighter plane.

"Well, my friend the American oil company man happened to be all hopped up with patriotism that morning. Anyway, looking this Lufthansa pilot in the eye coldly, he said he didn't have any of this gas for sale.

"'You mean you don't want to sell it to me?' says the Lufthansa pilot.

"'Maybe I mean that,' said the American oil company man.

"'I can entirely appreciate your sensibilities,' says the Lufthansa pilot, without flickering an eyelid. We stand there, watching him as he gets back into his plane—taxis two hundred yards down the field to the pumps of the British-owned and controlled Royal Dutch Shell. We see him get out and talk and two minutes later they're filling every tank in his plane with that same high-octane grade which the American refused to sell him."

Just then the American reporter for whom I had been waiting came in the door. With a casual word of farewell to the swarthy young man I crossed the room to my newspaper friend and we sat down at a table.

"Sorry you came so soon," I said. "I'd hoped to get myself picked up by a Gestapo agent."

"Looks like you're already fixed up. What's the matter with Schmidt?" And he nodded toward the swarthy young man who was just tipping the last of his Haig down his throat.

"Is he Gestapo? I thought it was a pretty clumsy pick-up."

"I wouldn't call Schmidt clumsy."

"He didn't get any information out of me."

"He didn't want any. That's not his department."

"What did he want?"

"He's a rumor-spreader. One of their best."

"What does he spread?"

"Whatever Berlin orders. Couldn't tell you what his line of goods is this week. When business is slack, Schmidt falls back on his staples—like the one about the American oil man who refused to sell gas to the Lufthansa."

"Is it true?"

"Hell, no. The American oil company he usually hangs it on hasn't even got a pump in Portugal. I checked up on it when he first started spreading it two months ago."

"What is the story supposed to prove?"

"Didn't it make you boiling mad at the British?"

"For a minute."

"Then I wouldn't say, if I were you, that the Gestapo was so clumsy and heavy-handed."

Back to Margaret at the hotel I sleep fitfully, waken to hear through the curtains the beautiful dawn noises of a Latin town. Carts clattering over cobblestones, the sounds mellowed by echoing between colored plaster walls. Then the street cries begin, like little fragments of an opera.

I've heard them many times before in other Latin countries, but every other time they wakened me with a tingle of romance. Now I only want to get this poor little kid away quick, into a shiny scrubbed world and away to some place where the milk isn't boiled. The quicker we scramble on the clipper, the better.

But at Panamerica's office they've never heard of me. I pick up Margaret and set her on the counter where the man can see her. Sure, it's a cheap one, but I'd use even cheaper tricks to get her away.

"Now look, I don't give a damn for myself. I'm a war

correspondent and used to it. But you know this country
is no place for a child. I'm not trying to pull anything—
I *do* have a reservation paid for months ago in New
York."

In the patient way he's needed to deal with so many
harassed, frightened people—the clerk repeats that there
is absolutely no record in this office yet—that people are
still here who've been waiting for months.

"Where do we go now, daddy?"

"Just down this street to a place where a man lives who
owns a ship that goes to America. Daddy's going to see if
the man will take us on his ship—because the man who
owns the airplane won't let us go."

"I want to go to Merika today."

Only we can't, because the steamship line also insists
they've never heard of us. Nothing to do now but cable
New York and wait for answers.

Down at the end of a side street glitters a wedge of
Lisbon harbor, framed between old renaissance buildings.

"Oh, look, daddy!"

"It's the ocean, darling, just like in England."

From the quai she stands squinting at the gulls wheeling over the sparkling water.

"Where do they keep the wire? The wire—where
is it?"

"Thy don't have any wire by the ocean here."

"When will they get some?"

"They don't need it. Because there isn't any war, Margaret. The wire in England was only to keep the Germans from coming in over the water. And in America they have fine beaches without any barbed wire, so you can go down and dig in the sand."

"I want to go today. You take me."

"Well, now we'll go back to the hotel and send some cables." But a block back up the street she stops again to point.

"Look, daddy—a sweet shop!" So it is—recognizable even in Portugal—the window crowded with little bowls of candy wrapped in tinfoil and colored papers. "You buy me a sweet."

"Well, daddy doesn't just know about sweets in Lisbon, Margaret. But we can come back tomorrow and see if we can find some that wouldn't hurt you."

"Why can't we today?"

"Because now we must send the cables."

"But tomorrow," persists Margaret, " 'haps the shop might be bombed."

At four o'clock the next afternoon a phone call comes from the steamship line. They've heard from New York, so it develops there is a single cabin open on the boat, which sails in only two hours, if I can make it. But they aren't sure it would be big enough for me and my daughter.

"Oh yes, it will. We're going to sail on that boat. She isn't my daughter—yet. She's a three-year-old English girl."

"Has she her Portuguese exit visa?"

"What the hell do you mean, exit visa?"

"We're very sorry. The Portuguese won't let her go unless she has an exit visa from their police. Technically she's a belligerent. All the Germans have to do the same."

"Hold that cabin," I shout. "I'll have the visa long before six o'clock."

They don't think I will, they explain, as it's a saint's birthday and police headquarters are closed. "And if you aren't aboard, you'll have to forfeit the money."

"That's my lookout," and I hang up.

Since Margaret is British, maybe her own consulate can help. And by one of those coincidences, barred from realistic fiction which often happen in real life, who do we find in the waiting room but Sir Somebody, coming out of the Minister's private office.

He comes over solicitously. I explain the problem and instantly, of course, anything our chaps can do, and can't he give me a chit to the Minister, or perhaps the press secretary? So presently things begin to hum. Margaret's big green passport disappears into a mass of cockney clerks. Messengers with the brass lion and unicorn insignia of Crown Messengers hastily depart, return and depart again. In half an hour they have located the police official in the bosom of his family, and my little belligerent has a smeary exit visa stamped on page three of the big green passport with her tiny smiling photograph.

By the time the sunset rays slant through the portholes of the dining saloon, Margaret and Babar and I are finishing her first glass of pineapple juice and we hear the rumble of anchor chains.

Thank God for a routine, and how a child loves it! We're up at eight, dressed and down to breakfast. Then we walk on deck until boullion in our deck chairs at ten. Then another walk until lunch and after this it's rest time. Margaret goes to bed in her bunk, I draw the curtains and leave the door just a crack open. Then I have a couple of hours' free time. At four, we're out on deck again. Her tea is at five—a tray in her deck chair, and she's usually back in bed for the night at six-thirty. By the time I'm up from my dinner to peek in the door at eight, she's usually asleep.

Margaret is very lonely. The boat is full of refugee children all chattering French, so she cannot join in their play. Another child of Margaret's age seems to be in her fix, a blonde youngster with milky blue eyes who plays alone and looks wistfully after us as we pass.

"What is your name?" I ask, but there is no answer.

[251]

"Comment t'apel-tu?" But she only stares, so she isn't French.

"Come si chiama?" Again the stare, so she isn't Italian. Then I guess. "Was heist du?"

"Ich. heis Gretchen." So I make the introductions both in English and in German, and after that Margaret and Gretchen are inseparable, giggling and romping on the deck, playing without the slightest need for words.

A group of 'teen age French girls, with big soft brown eyes, graceful as young gazelles, stop to play with Margaret, and one picks up Gretchen.

"And this little one, she is also yours?"

"No, she isn't."

"But she is American?"

"No, not American."

"English then?"

"Not English."

"But what is she?"

"A little German girl."

The big eyes widen in shocked surprise. "A-a-ah! Une p'tite Allema-a-ande!" Quickly Gretchen is set down on the deck and the French girls flutter off like horrified butterflies. Yet I can hardly blame them, fleeing from the gray armies which tramp their cities.

Gretchen's father, it develops, is in the German army. Her mother, dismally, constantly seasick, spends all days and evenings in her deck chair, pale eyes closed. Gretchen is badly neglected. When we are not on deck her only friends are two elderly placid couples of German Jews, whose deck chairs are near ours. They tell me the bombing in Cologne was terrible, and they sing little German nursery rhymes to Gretchen, see that she gets enough to eat, smile benignly as she plays. Even the war and persecution cannot disturb the sunset of what have been obviously happy, useful lives. But one of the Jewish women is indignant that Gretchen is so neglected, the little knitted dress so dirty.

"You must not think," she warns me sternly, "that *all* German mothers are like that. German women are very good to their children, and careful! One should not judge the many by the few!"

They all smile as Gretchen and Margaret laugh and roll on the deck in front of us, tangled in each other's arms.

One of the placid old Jews turns to me. "If only the statesmen of Europe were as sensible as the children!"

At last the shore line is gliding past the porthole. Very soon now we'll be in, and I've packed while Margaret is finishing her afternoon nap. Now I struggle with customs' declarations. Mine is simple because I'm allowed a hundred dollars' exemption. But Margaret as an alien has no such allowance. Everything must be listed. Not of course her nightie, or her toothbrush, or the pencil she

[253]

writes to Hedy with. Hardly her well-thumbed photo of Kathrine, because it was really mine. But probably her teddy bear and certainly the bomb. Because even though, since she got Babar, she doesn't need to sleep with it any more, it's indubitably hers because it fell in her back garden. And what else? Well, nothing. The little mite is traveling very light for a 3,000-mile trip. So on the customs form for alien declarations I list, after Margaret's name, her entire goods and chattels:

> 1 teddy bear (used)
> 1 2-lb. magnesium incendiary bomb case

And presently we are on the pier with Kathrine, Margaret staring at her with those big burning black eyes—very eager, taking in everything, but she still clings to me, and Kathrine doesn't want to force it.

"You stay here with Margaret and the baggage," she insists. "Give me the customs slips and I'll go bring an examiner."

Margaret stares after. "Why are her eyes like that?"

"They're blue eyes, darling."

"But why aren't they like mine?"

"Because yours are brown."

"But if she is mummy, why aren't her eyes brown?"

Only at this minute Kathrine comes running back. "Darling, you've got Margaret in trouble—what's this about a bomb on her customs declaration?"

"It's hers. It's only a magnesium case—"

"Will it go off?"

"Oh no. All the thermite has been poured out."

"Well, tell the customs man that, quick. They think Margaret's a spy, in here on a false passport to blow up the Port of New York. Here he comes now—that one with the bucket of water."

"Well, you keep Margaret. Margaret, will you stay with mummy?"

"Yes," says Margaret, and walks over to take her fore-finger in her small fist.

This story, since it is taken from the stuff of real life, would go on indefinitely if we did not end it here. No longer do we have to make the blackout in Margaret's room, closing every curtain tightly before she will go to sleep, as we did the first month. And she understands that nothing ever drops out of the shiny transport planes that glitter overhead, hardly looks up from her play as they buzz over Central Park on their way to La Guardia Field.

Sometimes old shadows rise, but they are not of the war. They are ghosts of mothers, real or foster but loved not the less for that, who suddenly went away for reasons which four-year-olds of course cannot understand. So even today:

"Mummy, why do you have your hat on?"

"I'm going out to do some shopping."

"But will you come back?"

"Of course, Margaret. You know now I always do."

"Will you really?"

"Yes, darling."

"Promise me your word?" And the desperate little eyes fill with tears.

"Of course, dear." But Margaret is inconsolable.

"Is that the truf?" she sobs piteously, looking upward. "Will I see?"

Slowly the old ghosts fade.